WALKING

— ON —

WATER

THE WEST PIER STORY

by

FRED GRAY

FOREWORD *by* ASA BRIGGS

© FRED GRAY 1998

THIS EDITION PUBLISHED IN GREAT
BRITAIN 1998 BY THE BRIGHTON
WEST PIER TRUST, THE WEST PIER,
KINGS ROAD, BRIGHTON, BN1 2FL

SPONSORED BY **SEEBOARD**

DESIGNED BY FRANK AINSCOUGH

A CIP CATALOGUE RECORD FOR THIS
BOOK IS AVAILABLE FROM THE BRITISH
LIBRARY.

PRINTED IN MALTA THROUGH
PRINTWORKS INT. LIMITED

ISBN 0 9504082 5 5

CONTENTS

PAGE FIVE

PREFACE & ACKNOWLEDGEMENTS

PAGE SEVEN

FOREWORD

by Asa Briggs

CHAPTER ONE ~ PAGE EIGHT

WALKING ON WATER

CHAPTER TWO ~ PAGE FOURTEEN

THE PROMENADE PIER

'a kind of butterfly upon the ocean'

CHAPTER THREE ~ PAGE THIRTY-FIVE

THE PLEASURE PIER

'in a holiday mood'

CHAPTER FOUR ~ PAGE FIFTY-SIX

THE FUNFAIR PIER

'all the fun of the fair'

CHAPTER FIVE ~ PAGE SEVENTY-SEVEN

THE CLOSED PIER

by Dr Geoff Lockwood

PREFACE &
ACKNOWLEDGEMENTS

Finding out about the West Pier was akin to doing a jig-saw puzzle with an infuriatingly large number of pieces missing and no picture to work from. There were many gaps in the previous accounts of the Pier's history and attempting to fit these together with other disparate pieces of information, opinion and memory was difficult because the material lacked a reasoned framework: the story simply did not add up.

Together with Mary Hoar and Pat Millward, I searched high and low in record offices, libraries and archives across the country for more substantial information. Usually this was a thankless task as little seemed to have survived about the Pier. A short time before they died I had long conversations with John Lloyd and Bryan Spielman, the two key people who fought to save the Pier after closure in 1975. Both provided fascinating insights into the Pier's recent history. John, however, despaired that the records of the West Pier Company had been destroyed in an act of vandalism, as he saw it, by the Official Receiver sometime after 1978.

It was therefore a wonderful surprise when Mary Hoar discovered in the East Sussex Record Office the superb, although incomplete, business records of the Company for the 1890s to 1960s. We owe a considerable debt to the staff of the Record Office not only for facilitating our use of the material but also for having the foresight to acquire the records - without them our understanding of the Pier would be far less. These records provide the backbone of *Walking on Water* around which we were able to reconstruct a surer history of the Pier.

The story of how and why the Pier was built is mostly derived from reports in the local and national press of the time. The tale of Brighton Swimming Club's relationship with the Pier Company comes from material kindly provided by David Sawyers. The account of the West Pier divers was pieced together from a variety of documentary sources and from conversations with a number of people including Zoe Brigden's son, John, and Ron Cunningham, better known as the Great Omani.

The section of *Walking on Water* about the transformation into a pleasure pier is largely drawn from a scrapbook of dozens of newspaper cuttings and Company reports from the 1890s, compiled at the time by some anonymous person and many decades later acquired by John Lloyd. Details of later entertainments in the Theatre and the Concert Hall come from Company records, programmes held by the West Pier Trust, newspaper reports and material in the Theatre Museum, Covent Garden.

For the inter-war years onwards we were fortunate to be able to hear from people who had been on the Pier in a variety of guises - for example, as holiday-makers, performers, stall-holders or soldiers. Their memories help bring the Pier's past alive and for the future I hope the West Pier Trust will be able to gather many more recordings of people recounting their personal histories of the Pier. Memories, though, play tricks and some people we spoke to were certain that they had seen plays in the Theatre, after the Second World War, although from the Company records we know this was not the case. In turn, however, the use of documentary evidence may also be problematic. Despite their richness, the Pier Company records were sometimes difficult to interpret and usually there was no-one we could turn to for an explanation.

The description of the decade of events that led to closure in 1975 is based in part on existing accounts published by the Trust, a reading of newspaper reports (especially from the *Evening Argus*) and conversations with John Lloyd. Geoff Lockwood wrote the final chapter about the dark age in the Pier's history that followed closure.

In developing an understanding of the Pier we were also able to draw on an abundance of visual material, from snapshots to architectural drawings. The Pier itself was a great resource, revealing layer upon layer of past times. Both the peeling signs for speedboat trips and the surviving grandeur of the Concert Hall were eerie reminders of what had gone before. I am indebted to Jon Orrell and his colleagues for taking me on journeys both under the Pier and underwater to view sights rarely seen by people walking above the waves.

The story told in *Walking on Water* is incomplete. There is much we still do not know about the Pier's past. As far as I am aware, only fragments remain of the original 1860s plans and drawings for the Pier and none survive for the 1916 Concert Hall. Eugenius Birch, the father of the Pier, remains a mysterious figure despite some excellent detective work by John Lloyd; no portrait of Birch seems to exist and his professional and personal papers appear not to have survived. We do not know the details of how the original structure was engineered, nothing of the Scottish foundry where the iron was made and we have few insights into the lives of the workers who built the Pier. I hope in the future these and other still missing pieces of the West Pier jigsaw will be re-discovered.

I am grateful to the numerous people and organisations who provided information and material about the Pier. Colleagues at the University of Sussex, including Sara Hinchliffe and Geoffrey Mead, helped in a number of ways. I owe a great debt to Mary Hoar for her immense commitment

to the *Walking on Water* project. Her research has been inspiring and her enthusiasm and humour unflagging.

Turning the story of the Pier into a book was made possible by sponsorship from Seeboard plc. My thanks to Seeboard and Chris English. I am indebted to Lord Briggs for writing the Foreword and providing comments on a draft of the text. Other people, including Rachel Clark, Carol Gray, Maureen Rawlinson and Adam Trimingham, helped in various ways to make the book more readable.

Finally, I hope that my children Jack and Holly will enjoy the story and, when with other Brightonians they walk on the restored West Pier, it will help them appreciate who and what has gone before.

The publisher would like to thank the following for kind permission to reproduce the illustrations as indicated:

Betty Dowsett: 76; Anne Howard: 110, 119-126; April Henebury: 26, 68; Patti Gale: 94; Tim Phillips: 105-107; Bob Smith: front and back cover photographs, 117, 118, 132-148; Vera Spratt: 75; Madeleine and John Taylor: 72, 74, 79-83, 85-90, 93, 96; Tom Martin: 112; Brighton Swimming Club: 25, 54; Hemsley Orrell Partnership: 8, 65, 116; Royal Pavilion, Libraries and Museums, Brighton and Hove: 11, 13, 15, 16, 18, 28, 30, 33, 40, 42, 47, 66, 78; Brighton and Hove Council: 113-115; © RCHME Crown Copyright: page 6, 97-104.

Other illustrations come from the collections of the Brighton West Pier Trust and Fred Gray. Every effort has been made to trace and acknowledge holders of copyright. The publisher regrets any unwitting infringement of copyright and, should there have been any errors or omissions, would be pleased to hear from copyright holders, so that they may be corrected in future editions of this book.

FOREWORD

*I*t is both a privilege and a pleasure to write a brief foreword to this absorbing and highly accessible account of the history of Brighton's West Pier which bears just the right title. The book is based on careful research, but everything that Fred Gray has discovered – and he has discovered much long lost to view – is effortlessly incorporated into a compelling text.

I have always loved piers, and twenty-one years ago I wrote a foreword to Simon Adamson's excellent book *Seaside Piers* published in association with the Victorian Society of which I am now President. Loving all piers, I have a particular love of the West Pier, a love which goes back long before I was Vice-Chancellor of the University of Sussex and became associated with the struggle to retain it. There has always been a struggle. Piers are places of delight but the effort to conserve them is relentless. Far too many have gone. Those that remain are among the richest elements in our heritage.

In itself their architecture is fascinating. So, too, is the aesthetics, bound up with style as well as with function – and, above all, with fun. Yet it has never been possible at any stage in their history, to separate aesthetics from economics. Piers have at least to pay for themselves. Seldom have they made great profits. They belong in a real sense to the people who use them. They are part of our social as well as our architectural heritage. For the social historian, interested both in work and in leisure – and there are far more of them around than there were in 1977 – piers are unique witnesses to changing ways of life. And because those piers that remain are in danger, in pleading for any particular one we always have to think of its future and the opportunities that it offers, not just of the past. The West Pier has a great future when the danger disappears.

It is a privilege to write this foreword because I am proud to have been associated with the struggle for the West Pier in more than one phase and because I admire the determination and enterprise of the people who have led that struggle and have sought a realistic but imaginative outcome. Fred Gray tells an unfinished story. As Geoffrey Lockwood, indefatigable in his efforts, explains in the final pages of this book, telling the last chapter in the story, we trust that there will be a new volume of history to come. I hope that Fred Gray will write it.

ASA BRIGGS
MARCH 1998

CHAPTER ONE

WALKING ON WATER

1 ◇ THE PROMENADE PIER WITH OPEN
DECK, KIOSKS AND WEATHER SCREENS
AT THE PIER HEAD

2 ◇ BRIGHTON AS THE WEST PIER.
THE COVER OF THE BRIGHTON OFFICIAL
HANDBOOK 1934-35, DESIGNED BY
HG GAWTHORN

Brighton's West Pier is an exceptional seaside pier. Although long closed and abandoned to the elements, miraculously it still survives as a symbolic part of seaside England and an enduring feature of the Brighton seafront.

A classic pleasure pier, the West Pier was built with its root end anchored in the dry land of the seafront, with the main part of the structure gliding over the wave-washed pebbles and out above the sea. Part of the enchantment of the Pier is that it uses but transcends three environments. It rests on the seabed, but is not part of the sea; it comes from the land, but is landless; it is in the air, but is not airborne.

The West Pier opened on 6 October 1866 and was one of dozens built around the coast of England and Wales, in the great era of pier construction, during the second half of the nineteenth century. The Pier reveals the skills and talents of the Victorian engineer as mechanic, architect and artist using materials and technologies developed from the industrial revolution. As an archetypal resort building, the Pier combined functional engineering for the marginal and hostile sea-shore environment with a fantasy of performance architecture to entertain visitors.

Dozens of iron piles, screwed into the seabed, provided the Pier's foundations. Iron columns attached to these piles rose above the sea, linked by a mesh of metal ties, braces and girders. The simple iron framework allowed waves to sweep through and around the Pier, rather than crash against the structure, and provided the strength to support the superstructure of decking, entertainment buildings and associated paraphernalia including seats and shelters. On the wooden promenade deck visitors could seemingly be at sea and walk on water without the hazards of getting wet or being sea sick. Pier building, however, was as much an art as an exact science and the original structure occasionally 'oscillated' in an alarming fashion, creating panic among visitors who feared it would collapse and pitch them into the sea – strengthening work was necessary to remove the threat to the Pier. From the deck up the West Pier was seaside performance architecture at its finest, designed to entice visitors on to the Pier and entertain holiday-makers once there. The relatively simple building designs, based around metal frames covered by timber, were hidden by the surface architectural finery which included a host of images – human faces, dolphins, shields, urns and garlands – oriental minarets, intricate cast iron railings and seats, and serpent lamp posts, all typical of English seaside frippery and pomp.

Just as piers became symbolic of the British seaside resort – few were without at least one – so the West Pier became a major emblem of Brighton portrayed on endless postcards and, particularly during the inter-war years, featuring on guidebook covers and posters advertising the town. The West Pier story is the history in microcosm of the English seaside holiday since the mid-nineteenth century. Built as a speculative venture, the success of the enterprise depended on attracting sufficient visitors spending enough money to generate income for the upkeep of the Pier and profits for the West Pier Company. As holiday-making changed, so the Pier Company

3 ❖ THE PLEASURE PIER AT THE TURN OF THE CENTURY WITH PAVILION, LANDING STAGES AND CENTRAL BANDSTAND

responded by adapting and developing the Pier. The Pier provided seaside holiday experiences – sometimes quiet and sedate, sometimes exciting and out of this world – for millions of people. It was a place of work for thousands of others, from actors, musicians and professional divers to stall holders, waitresses, amusement arcade attendants and deck hands.

Despite their earlier grandeur and importance, relatively few seaside piers escaped the twentieth century unscathed. Many have been swept away by storm, destroyed by fire, or demolished as unsafe or uneconomic. Those that remain are mostly shadows of their former selves, either truncated in length or radically altered or re-built in response to the changing demands of holiday industries and fashions in leisure and pleasure. A few of the latter, such as Blackpool's Central Pier and Brighton's Palace Pier are successful offshore funfairs and theme parks. Of the minority that have survived architecturally unchanged some, such as Clevedon Pier, are open decked with no significant pier buildings.

By the narrowest of margins and through inactivity and indecision rather than design, the West Pier escaped this pervasive sweep of destruction, change and redevelopment. As a classic pleasure pier it is unique in retaining its original buildings: there have been no substantial changes or additions since the First World War. Despite being developed over half a century, the overall form and coherence of the West Pier make it one of the finest remaining examples of nineteenth and early twentieth century seaside architecture. Acclaimed as 'the Queen of Piers', its individual buildings are also exceptional – the Theatre and Concert Hall are two of the most important surviving Victorian and Edwardian seaside entertainment buildings. In 1982 the West Pier was listed architecturally as a Grade I building, the only pier to be so distinguished.

When opened in 1866, the Pier was one of the first with the prime function of promenading rather than being a landing stage bridging ship and shore. As a space to promenade over the sea, the Pier was a place for the Victorian middle-classes to socialise, see and be seen, exhibit their wealth, consume the health-giving properties of sea air, and take in panoramic views of sea and coast. The early Pier was an exceptional artificial environment where the sea, air and view could all be consumed, in supposed comfort and safety, while maintaining the social conventions of dress and behaviour. The original Pier was an open deck structure – the only buildings were two toll houses at the entrance, six small 'ornamental houses' or kiosks along the deck and protective weather screens at the pier head. Probably drawing on the oriental style of Brighton's Royal Pavilion, the kiosks were some of the first specially designed pier pleasure buildings, providing the inspiration for many later seaside buildings. There were also ramps for bath chair access from the promenade to the level deck of the Pier – an early example of design for people with physical disabilities.

4 ⊕ THE PLEASURE PIER BETWEEN THE WARS. THE PIER REMAINS FUNDAMENTALLY UNCHANGED SINCE THE COMPLETION OF THE CONCERT HALL IN 1916

During the 1890s the West Pier began to be transformed from a promenade pier into a pleasure pier. The pier head was widened and strengthened, becoming the location for a large pavilion, with an oriental exterior design, opened in 1893 and converted into a theatre a decade later. Landing stages for the pleasure steamer trade were constructed around the pier head and another major building midway along the Pier – the Concert Hall – was completed in 1916. The pleasure pier had a great variety of seaside entertainments both indoors and out. Attractions included the Pier's own orchestra and military bands playing in the Concert Hall, an all year round programme of plays, musicals and pantomimes in the Theatre, aquatic entertainers and professional divers, paddle steamer excursions and public swimming from the bathing station at the pier head. In its pleasure pier heyday, the West Pier was a hugely popular palace of seaside entertainment visited by over two million people each year.

Between the wars the pleasure pier enterprise waned and visitor numbers dropped below the million. In response, the Pier Company introduced new funfair attractions, including a miniature motor racing track at the entrance to the Pier. Wartime dangers, including the threat of invasion, closed the Pier for much of the Second World War, but with the post-war re-opening the evolution into a funfair pier was completed. The Concert Hall became a café and the Theatre was converted into the Ocean Restaurant upstairs and the 'Laughterland' games pavilion downstairs. Visitors could enjoy fairground stalls and amusement arcades, a crazy mirror maze and a helter-skelter, speedway racing, dodgems and a ghost train and, by the 1950s, a juke-box.

But the funfair attractions were not a complete response to the challenges of the post-war era and the Pier continued a slow decline. Grand plans for revival came to nothing; in 1970 the pier head was sealed off as dangerous and the remainder of the Pier was closed to the public on 30 September 1975. As the threat to the West Pier mounted, so did the concern and action of people wishing to save it and in 1978 the West Pier Trust became its owner.

With closure the Pier became increasingly derelict and ruined, a forlorn sight eventually cut off from the land and at risk of being swept away

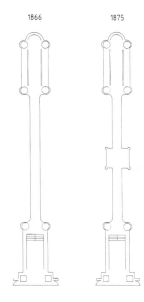

1866   1875

by sea and storm or demolished. The home of pigeons and starlings rather than a palace of seaside fun and entertainment, the derelict island Pier could conjure powerful and sometimes conflicting images. For some people it was romantic and picturesque, perhaps invoking wistful memories of past holiday pleasures, while for others the Pier was decrepit and ruined, an emphatic symbol of the decline of Brighton and the English seaside resort.

Perhaps perversely, closure, decay and threatened demolition strengthened the Pier's popular appeal and appreciation of its architectural glories. As the twentieth century drew to a close, there appeared an increasing likelihood that the Pier would be saved. In 1996 the Heritage Lottery Fund awarded the Trust almost £1 million for emergency work to stabilise the structure. Plans were prepared to rejuvenate the Pier, reinstating the exterior to its 1920s heyday and offering imaginative new attractions for twenty-first century visitors. In this vision, dependent on lottery and private finance, the West Pier will once more be a major economic asset in a town blighted by unemployment, and be restored as the vibrant, sparkling jewel of the Brighton seafront. ⊱

Opposite top and below

5 AND 6 ✧ THE FUNFAIR PIER

7 ✧ THE DERELICT PIER

8 ✧ THE EVOLVING PIER 1866 – 1994, STAGES OF DEVELOPMENT

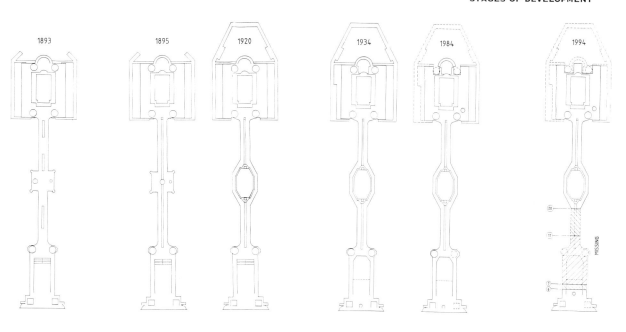

THE PROMENADE PIER

'a kind of butterfly upon the ocean'

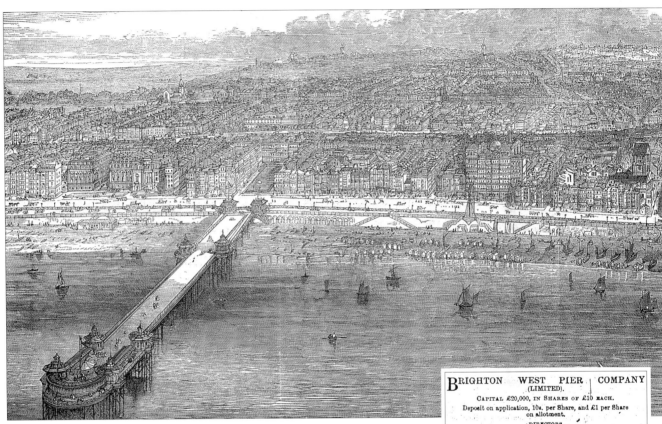

9 ✧ A BIRD'S EYE VIEW OF THE
PROMENADE PIER PUBLISHED IN
AUGUST 1872 AND SHOWING THE
'AMPLE AND CONTINUOUS SEAT-ACCOM-
MODATION' ON THE PIER HEAD

10 ✧ 'A HANDSOME, COMMODIOUS AND
SUBSTANTIAL IRON PROMENADE PIER...'
THE ABRIDGED PROSPECTUS FOR THE
BRIGHTON WEST PIER COMPANY PUB-
LISHED IN SUMMER 1863

BRIGHTON WEST PIER COMPANY
(LIMITED).

CAPITAL £20,000, IN SHARES OF £10 EACH.

Deposit on application, 10s. per Share, and £1 per Share
on allotment.

DIRECTORS.

Mr Henry Moor, 5, Clarendon-terrace, Brighton (Chairman).
Mr William Coningham, M.P., 26, Sussex-square, Brighton.
Mr W. Grover Ashby, 21, Silwood-street, Brighton.
Mr Thomas Crunden, New-road, Brighton.
Mr Joseph Ellis, King's-road, Brighton.
Mr Henry Smithers (Alderman), 21, Buckingham-place, Brighton.

BANKERS.

London and County Bank, Hanover-square, London, and Brighton
Branch.

ENGINEER.

Mr E. BIRCH, M.I.C.E., 43, Parliament-street, London, S.W.

SOLICITOR AND SECRETARY.

Mr W. H. SIMPSON, 38, Parliament-street, London, S.W.

ABRIDGED PROSPECTUS.

The object of this Company is to erect a handsome, commodious,
and substantial Iron Promenade Pier, opposite Regency-square, in
the centre of that portion of the Esplanade which, at all seasons of
the year, is the most thronged by residents and visitors.

Assuming that on the average one-half of the annual visitors to
Brighton would visit the Pier once during their stay, an income
equal to upwards of 13 per cent. on the Capital, would be derived by
the Company.

From the above and other sources it is calculated, a Dividend of at
least 15 per cent. may be safely anticipated.

The amount of each call will not exceed £2 per share, and there
will be a clear interval of two months between each call.

Deposits paid on unallotted shares will be returned in full.

Prospectuses and Forms of Applications for Shares may be
obtained of the Secretary, or of the Company's Local Agent, Mr
Joseph Cordwell, 79, West-street, Brighton.

As the Share List will shortly close, an early application is recommended.

*A*ll morning on Saturday 6 October 1866 that 'terrible visitation, a long-enduring, persistent sea-side drizzle' had threatened to envelop Brighton. But the drizzle held off and the thousands of people who had gathered on the sea front for the ceremony and celebrations marking the opening of Brighton's new Pier stayed dry. By early afternoon 'the balconies of the houses were crowded with well-dressed ladies, the King's Road was lined with equipages and pedestrians, and the shore thronged with people'. The new Pier, packed with invited guests and the first visitors paying the premium admission fee of one shilling, was decorated with flags from all nations. The older Chain Pier was decked with bunting. On the Pier itself, music was provided by the band of the 68th Light Infantry Regiment from Portsmouth.

At two o'clock a procession marched from the pier head to the entrance of the Pier. It included the Chief Constable and inspectors of the police, two bands, 50 Coastguards with drawn cutlasses, the contractors' workmen carrying flags and banners, the Mayor and other Brighton Corporation dignitaries, Members of Parliament, directors and officers of the Brighton Railway Company and a full complement of people involved in the construction of the Pier – the contractors, the engineer and Chairman, directors and officers of the West Pier Company. Opening speeches were made from the raised and carpeted dais near the entrance gates. Mr Henry Moor, the Chairman of the West Pier Company, declared the Pier open and the Mayor replied on behalf of Brighton Corporation. The procession returned to the pier head, Mr Moor again announced the Pier was open, the Royal Standard was hoisted up the flag staff on the pier head, and 'a gun detachment of the Coast Guard saluted it with 21 guns, fired from a couple of 9-pounders in the centre of the Pier'.

Starting at four o'clock an inauguration dinner, attended by 140 dignitaries, took place in the Banqueting Room at the Royal Pavilion. There were congratulatory speeches and toasts. Meanwhile, the foremen and workmen were feasted at the Bedford Hotel. The planned conclusion to the celebrations was the illumination of the Pier throughout the evening and a 'grand display of fireworks'.

The ceremonial pomp and festivities were excellent publicity and there was detailed coverage of the opening of the Pier in national and local news-

Opposite top

11 ✧ **An early engraving of 'The New Pier' showing its relationship to Regency Square and the large expanse of promenading space**

Opposite below

12 ✧ **An artist's impression of the new Pier, 'The Illustrated Times', April 1865, eighteen months before the Pier opened**

13 ✧ **The Mayor of Brighton and Mr Henry Moor, the Chairman of the West Pier Company, declaring the Pier open**

papers. The inaugural events also reveal the considerable and confident expectations for the new Pier. Unsurprisingly, Henry Moor, as Chairman of the Pier Company, believed 'this noble structure stands unrivalled throughout the whole of Europe' and that 'the town of Brighton has gained...one of the noblest structures, one of the most splendid erections, that can form an adjunct to any town in England'. For Mr J Locke, MP and Recorder of Brighton, the Pier 'was a kind of butterfly upon the ocean to carry visitors upon its wings and waft them amongst the zephyrs and balmy breezes of Brighton'. The Mayor 'trusted that the Pier would ever remain a benefit to the town, that the elements above and below it would be propitious; and that the healthy and sick, the rich and the humble, might alike enjoy the health-inspiring breezes to be obtained upon it; and that the weak might be restored to robust health. He hoped that the Pier might remain to future ages to prove what speculation had done'. The press agreed with such sentiments, *The Brighton Examiner*, for instance, arguing 'we now look upon the structure as artistic and elegant, outrivalling everything of the kind in this country, and perhaps the world'.

The new Pier was a speculative venture, built to attract visitors able and willing to pay to promenade on its deck. The enterprise depended on selling the Pier as an exclusive and unique promenade experience to enough people to cover the Company's costs and make a profit. As the abridged prospectus for the Company published in the summer of 1863 stated, the object 'is to erect a handsome, commodious, and substantial Iron Promenade Pier...in the centre of that portion of the Esplanade which, at all seasons of the year, is the most thronged by residents and visitors'. The Company believed that sufficient visitors would be attracted that 'a Dividend of at least 15 per cent, may be safely anticipated'.

OPENING OF THE WEST PIER, BRIGHTON.

The New Pier, Brighton, No.1.

14 ❖ THE OPENING CELEBRATIONS
SATURDAY 6 OCTOBER 1866

A major Victorian leisure time activity, promenading was much more than just walking. The West Pier, and other Victorian promenade piers, was designed as an exclusive extension to the seafront, providing a safe, family centred, middle-class and regulated space. The Pier gave access to controlled promenading where people could walk and rest, be seen, meet and talk with other people, breathe the healthy sea air and take in views of both nature and society. Promenading was an essentially passive pleasure to be enjoyed by individuals who were also members – and keen to be so – of the holiday crowd.

Making a success of the speculative promenade venture depended on a number of factors. The Pier needed to be safe, secure and exclusive. It required space for walking and facilities for resting. It had to offer additional attractions that distinguished it from the normal seafront promenade. The new Pier excelled in meeting most although not quite all of these demands.

The Pier was designed by the great Victorian pier engineer Eugenius Birch (1818 – 1884). Active during the height of pier-building mania, Birch was responsible for more than a dozen seaside piers from Margate Jetty in 1853 to Plymouth Pier in 1884, as well as aquaria in Brighton and Scarborough, Exmouth docks and Ilfracombe harbour. It was Birch who made

popular the innovative 'worm' or screw piling technique – originally patent-ed in the 1830s by Alexander Mitchell as part of a floating dry dock invention – used in many piers of countless shapes and designs constructed in the second half of the nineteenth century. One of the breed of creative Victori-an engineers, Birch's pier work required engineering, architectural and design knowledge combined with vision, imagination and artistry.

The firm of Laidlaw and Son, of Glasgow, won the contract for erec-tion of the Pier for £21,890. Laidlaw's built a number of other piers during the 1860s including Blackpool North and Central, Deal, Lytham, Rhyl and Hastings. The component parts for the Pier were made in Glasgow, shipped round the coast and unloaded at Shoreham. Many of the men building the West Pier came from the just completed Deal Pier, another venture involv-ing both Birch and Laidlaw.

Construction of the new Pier (at this stage sometimes called the West-ern Pier, West End Pier or New Pier) started at the end of March 1864. It took two and a half years to complete, not the originally estimated six to twelve months. The explanation given by Laidlaw's for the long delay involved problems in shipping the components from Glasgow. They eventually promised to use rail rather than sea for transport, although it is likely that

15 ❖ THE PIER AT LOW TIDE SHOWING THE MASS OF SLENDER COLUMNS SUP-PORTING THE PIER'S SUPERSTRUCTURE

16 ✠ Before the Pier was finished residents of Regency Square complained that the toll houses would destroy their sea view

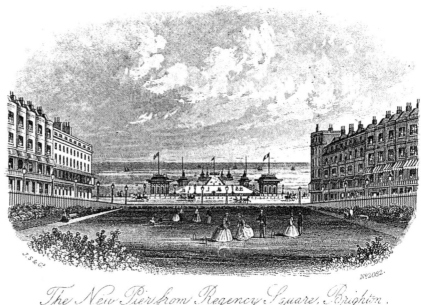

The New Pier from Regency Square, Brighton.

Laidlaw's themselves delayed completing the contract, probably because a large increase in the price of iron made the contracted price uneconomic. The final costs did massively exceed the contracted sum. The West Pier Company also experienced financial difficulties, and in August 1866, just two months before the new Pier opened, the original Company was dissolved and reincorporated with the power to increase its capital from £25,000 to £35,000.

17 ✠ The Chain Pier

Eugenius Birch, was the person behind the original intention to construct a new pier in Brighton. Birch's plan was to demolish the pioneering 1823 Chain Pier and to replace it with a new and modern structure. The owners of the Chain Pier refused and the old pier survived until 1896. A number of alternative locations were considered by Birch and other proponents of the new pier and the site facing Regency Square, a mile to the west of the Chain Pier, was eventually selected.

Comparison of the two piers shows both the changing purpose of seaside piers and the advances in pier building technology over 40 years. The Chain Pier is notable as one of the first seaside resort piers in England. At a time when Brighton was on an important cross-channel route, its principal purpose was as a landing stage (the alternative was an expensive and hazardous journey from beach to ship on the backs of boatmen and in rowing boats) although the Pier was also designed as a place of entertainment and promenade. The Chain Pier was built on wooden piles driven into the seabed. These provided the foundations for four cast iron towers carrying huge chains from which the 13-foot wide deck of the Pier hung suspended.

Although much the same length, at its narrowest point the West Pier was four times wider than the Chain Pier. It was constructed using a new pier building technology radically different from that used for the Chain Pier. The professional journal, *The Engineer*, at the time described how 'The ordinary process of pile-driving has been dispensed with: the iron pillars being screwed into the rocky sea-bed'. Iron piles with a huge screw thread at one end were literally screwed into the chalk beneath the seabed, using muscle power, to provide the foundations for the pier. On the other end of the piles were attached circular iron columns,

18 ❖ A STROLL ON THE PIER ON A SUNNY LATE AFTERNOON

19 ⟡ THE OPEN BANDSTAND AT THE PIER HEAD AND GHOSTLY IMAGES OF VICTORIAN PROMENADERS CAPTURED IN A PHOTOGRAPH OF 1870

which rose to a suitable height above the surface of the sea. The whole network of columns was linked together by a lattice of diagonal ties, rods and braces topped with horizontal girders providing a platform carrying the pier deck.

At the opening of the Pier commentators were concerned to stress the design strengths of the structure: '...columns and piles are braced and tied in such a manner as to ensure the greatest amount of stiffness to the Pier, and least amount of resistance to the sea'. For the Pier's piling and columns use was made of both slender solid wrought iron pillars, just four inches in diameter, and more substantial hollow cast iron tubes. Wrought iron is malleable and has tensile strength and elasticity; cast iron is less elastic and more resistant to corrosion.

The innovative construction technology was relatively untried and untested; pier building itself was an art as much as a science. After more than a century it is difficult to untangle the early engineering history of the Pier, although additional work was carried out on the structure on a number of occasions during the two decades after opening. Some later commentators argue that corrosion was a major difficulty, with the wrought iron piles being reduced to just a two-inch diameter within a few years and being replaced with less corrosive cast iron tubes. This seems unlikely since during emergency works in 1997 some original wrought iron piles were recovered in a remarkably good condition and part of the pier head was still supported by cast iron columns resting on original thinner solid wrought iron piles (the latter being visible at low tide).

A more likely explanation for the repeated works on the Pier in the two decades after its opening is that the wrought iron piles and inadequate ties and braces linking the columns allowed too much movement. This caused the Pier to vibrate, scaring visitors and forcing the Company to undertake remedial work on the structure. The mystery remains, however, as to whether from the outset Birch designed and engineered the structure to make use of wrought iron piles supporting cast iron columns or whether the cast iron was added subsequently to rectify earlier design inadequacies which had produced instability in the structure.

In contrast to the Chain Pier, the landing stage function of the West Pier was unimportant. The coming of the railway to Sussex in the 1840s had created alternative routes to France which bypassed Brighton. Although underneath the pier head were 'graduated landing stages to suit all times of the tide', they were used only for pleasure excursions by steamer. It was not until 30 years later that proper landing stages were built, also for the pleasure steamer trade. The railways, though, did lead to a new influx of visitors to holiday in the town who might be enticed to promenade on a new pier.

Unlike the suspension method used for the Chain Pier, the new technology meant that in theory the Pier could be any combination of

20 ✧ THE PROMENADE PIER AND IN THE FOREGROUND BOATS, BATHING MACHINES AND BENCHES ON THE BEACH

width and angle. It was an ideal means of extending the seafront promenade over the sea and creating large expanses of unhindered and open space
above the sea. From its root on the Brighton promenade to the south end
of the pier head, the length of the new Pier was 1,115 feet. At a low spring
tide the depth of water at the pier head today is eight feet, and at exceptionally low tides it is possible for a tall person to wade through the sea
beyond the southern end of the pier head. The width of the Pier ranged
from 265 feet at the landward end to 55 feet for much of its length before
broadening out to the 140-foot wide pier head.

Space was the most obvious requirement for promenading, something
the new Pier offered in abundance when compared to the Chain Pier. According to contemporary reports, the large area of open deck for walking made
'altogether over 100,000 superficial feet of promenade'. The pier head alone
was 140 feet wide and 310 feet long, an area of 39,000 square feet. At the
centre of the pier head was a small open platform used for band performances. The deck of the Pier was of close planking covered by 'gravel laid
upon bitumen' and this, rather than spaced timbers which became more
usual in subsequent decades, may have contributed to the instability of the
early Pier.

The West Pier promenaders were select and respectable. Standards of
behaviour were carefully regulated. (Even during the 1930s there was a
strict dress code for people promenading on the pier deck, although in the
early morning male bathers from the pier head could enjoy the sea naked,
unencumbered by costumes.) Admission to the Pier was by payment of a
toll of two pence, reduced to one penny on Sundays. The entrance to the
Pier was guarded by turnstiles, ornamental iron gates and two imposing
identical square toll houses in Italianate style. The unwanted were kept out
by money, architecture and social convention.

The toll houses were the most contentious feature of the new Pier. In
1865 the residents of Regency Square which overlooked the Pier, a number
of town councillors (not all, since some were also shareholders in the West
Pier Company) and commentators in the press protested that the toll houses
were too large, 'completely destroying the beautiful sweep of the bay, viewed
from the shore'. One press critic argued 'no beauty of structure can com-

pensate for the loss of sea view'. There were heated debates in meetings of the Town Council, Vestry and Pier Company: had permission for the toll houses been given by the Lords of the Manor and the Council; could or should they be demolished; were they for more than just the collection of tolls; would they add value to the Pier and houses in Regency Square; were they elegant; did they destroy the view of the sea; and would they be a credit to the town and attraction to visitors? The toll houses were far larger than similar structures on earlier piers and probably the largest pier buildings built to that date. The West Pier Company denied that the two buildings were for anything other than the collection of tolls, explaining that their size was part of the overall design for the whole Pier. Once the Pier opened the toll houses were used as shops, the only ones in such a prominent position on the beach side of the esplanade.

Although many subsequent piers, and at a later stage the West Pier itself, were to carry far larger and dominating pier buildings, the primary characteristic of the new Pier was its open promenade deck. However, the Pier also had some innovative and distinctive architectural features designed to capitalise on the nature of promenading and the mid-Victorian seaside holiday.

There was 'ample and continuous seat-accommodation', including the classic curved cast iron pier bench seating (identical to that on Birch's slightly later Eastbourne Pier) along the edge of the Pier, 'for 2,000 to 3,000 persons', facing inwards rather than outwards over the sea, allowing visitors to the Pier to rest, talk and look. The side of the Pier also carried railings and superb cast iron gas lamp standards in a serpent design. Both the long neck of the Pier and the broader pier head provided visitors with the illusion of being on a ship. There were untrammelled panoramic views out to sea and along the coast westwards to Worthing (and the slightly older Worthing Pier) and eastwards to the chalk cliffs towards Newhaven. Visitors could also enjoy the sight of crowded beaches and people using bathing machines at the water's edge. Along the sea-front the grand Regency terraces of Hove stretched into the distance while close to the Pier were Brighton's imposing new seaside hotels – the Grand, opened in 1864, and the Metropole, completed in 1890.

The Pier and its architecture also attempted to address the Victorian preoccupation with health. At least in public, respectable Victorians rarely conceded that their primary concern at the seaside was leisure or pleasure alone: these had to be combined with more rational pursuits including health and education. By the middle of the century belief in the curative properties of sea water, so often trumpeted in the eighteenth century, had given way to a conviction that the most beneficial aspects of the seaside came from breathing in sea air . Ozone was the thing – to be had on the promenade, but even more invigorating and health inducing when consumed directly above the sea. Middle class holiday makers were, however, eager to guard against exposure to other aspects of the natural environment: men and particularly women sought to protect their white skins from the sun, and it was not until the inter-war years of the twentieth century that sunbathing and suntans became popular.

The West Pier provided innovative ornamental weather screens on three sides of the pier head. The distinctive architecture of the screens represented design for health, comfort and social mixing. The screens were made of plate glass and cast iron, roofed over but open at the sides, with a

21 ◊ MILITARY FASHION UPON THE PIER

'line of double raised seats' either side of the screens. Commentators at the opening of the Pier thought the weather screens were especially important. They could not 'fail to be productive of a great comfort to the frequenters of the pier...[for]...on a sunny winter's day invalids can enjoy the mild temperature and life-prolonging air with perfect freedom from chilling blasts.... In summer the screens will shade the visitors from the sun without putting up an awning, which gives closeness and an air of confinement. It might be thought that with all this shelter the head of the pier would be confined in appearance. Nothing, however, could well be more open. The manner in which Mr Birch has obtained the maximum of accommodation and weather protection with the minimum of air-stoppage and light-obstruction, is a charming specimen of engineering skill.... As a sanatorium, this part of the Pier must be productive of the most beneficial effects to invalids and persons of delicate constitution'.

Although the sanatorium function of the innovative weather screens rather quickly seems to have been forgotten, the design was much copied in the architecture of many subsequent piers, with weather screens providing protection for visitors walking the length of a pier in bad weather. Within 30 years large sections of the West Pier screens had been dismantled and re-erected along the neck of the Pier.

Another feature of the Pier's architecture also proved to have a lasting reflection in pier design elsewhere. This was the inclusion of the six 'ornamental houses' integral to the deck of the Pier – perhaps the first example of substantial buildings on the body of a pier and the embryonic form of the pavilions and halls that became characteristic of many piers towards the end of the century. Two of the houses faced each other as the Pier narrowed from root end to the long pier neck, and the other four were at each corner of the broad expanse of the pier head. The design may have been inspired by the oriental exterior of the Brighton's Royal Pavilion. For example, the roof of each kiosk was topped by a small minaret surrounded by ornate railings. The six ornamental houses were used when individuals wanted to leave the promenade crowd. The two kiosks at the root end were for 'for toy and fancy businesses, and available for shelter'. The next two houses were to be 'used as refreshment rooms', while those at the seaward end were to be 'used severally as ladies' and gentlemen's retiring and lounging rooms'. Each of the kiosks also contained 'a spiral staircase leading to the roof, whence a magnificent panoramic view of the town, east and west, is obtained'.

The new Pier quickly became an important part of seaside Brighton. The one potentially ruinous flaw in the early years was the instability of the structure. One of the worst instances of the Pier moving was at 8.30 on the evening of Sunday 2nd August 1868. Panic broke out among the crowd on the pier head who feared the structure would collapse. A flurry of reports and letters in the local and national press described the incident. One letter writer to *The Times* explained the Pier was crowded, 'there being several thousand present at the head of the pier, many seated round, while others were standing and promenading during the performance of a band. There was a sudden commotion among the company, who endeavoured en masse to make for the shore end of the pier, ladies fainting and children screaming, some trodden upon, many of whom, I fear, must have been seriously injured. The cry having been raised that the pier was giving way was the cause of what might have proved a great calamity'.

Some people thought the movement resulted from a squall lifting the

22 ❖ **A LATE VICTORIAN PROMENADE.**
THE METROPOLE HOTEL OPENED IN 1890

decking. Others believed the problem arose from steamers using the
graduated landing stages built into
the pier head – a correspondent to
The Times described how in the previous year he had seen the
commander of a steamer, the *Albert
Victor*, using the pier to turn the
vessel on a spring. The manoeuvre
completed, 'suddenly the strain on
the pier ceased, and the pier oscillated in an alarming manner'. An
alternative explanation is that the
large crowd was so entranced by the

23 ✦ BY THE EARLY 1890S VISITORS
WALKING ON THE PIER WERE SHEL-
TERED BY A WEATHER SCREEN RUNNING
ALONG THE PIER NECK

rhythmic music of the band playing on the pier head that it began to march
in step, setting up an undulating ripple across the gravel and bitumen covered close planking and leading to consternation among the visitors.

Mr Welsford, the Secretary of the West Pier Company, sought to dispel
the concern, announcing 'the structure is in every way perfectly secure'.
Birch, as engineer of the Pier, added that 'the construction of the Pier is not
upon the principle of absolute rigidity, but provides for deflection, as essen-
tial to the security of such a structure as the Brighton West Pier'. Despite
these entreaties, the instability threatened the popularity of the Pier and in
turn the speculative venture. Works were carried out in the late 1860s and
again in 1874 and the mid-1880s to make the structure more stable.

For some critics, such as the naturalist Richard Jefferies, the normal
promenade experience was rather staid and tedious: 'Most people who go
on the West Pier at Brighton walk at once straight to the farthest part. This
is the order and custom of pier promenading; you are to stalk along the
deck until you reach the end, and there you go round and round the band
in a circle like a horse tethered to an iron pin, or else sit down and admire
those who do go round and round'.

Perhaps in response to such opinions and certainly in an attempt to
attract more visitors, the West Pier Company sought to improve the Pier.

The graduated landing stages were replaced by more substantial steps in 1885 and steamer excursions became a more important part of the Pier's business. Visitors and the Pier's entertainers were also offered more protection from the elements. In 1875 work started to widen the centre of the neck of the Pier and build a small but ornate covered bandstand, opened in 1877, at last providing some shelter for the previously exposed musicians. In 1888 a covered orchestra stand with moveable awnings to shelter the audience was constructed in the middle of the pier head.

The Company also sought to enliven the Pier experience with public spectacles using the sea. The Pier became a place for visitors to marvel at human ingenuity in conquering the watery elements, most typically through watching swimming and diving competitions and matches, individual demonstrations of physical prowess, stamina and ingenuity in the sea, and other displays that were more theatrical in performance, often with a strong pinch of comedy. Such swimming and diving spectacles in deep water were seen as an extraordinarily daring 'art', the preserve of a hardy and skilled few – mostly local people rather than visitors – and unique and exceptional activities that defied the conventional boundaries between people and the sea. In the mid-nineteenth century most seaside holiday-makers still did no more than bathe on the shoreline; they rarely went out of their depth, usually grasping the security of ropes tethered to bathing machines at the water's edge.

Soon after the Pier's opening the West Pier Company developed an important relationship with the Brighton Swimming Club that was sustained for over three decades. For the Swimming Club not only was the Pier an ideal venue and means of making swimming more popular, but the Pier Company also provided publicity and many of the cups, medals and cash prizes for races. On some occasions the West Pier Master, Captain Poland, acted as judge. For the Pier Company the 'aquatic entertainment' or 'aquatic sports' provided by the Swimming Club were a significant extra Pier attraction. By 1875 the Swimming Club's West Pier swimming matches 'attracted a large crowd of spectators .... Swimming in Brighton is comparatively a new thing, for it dates from 1860 when the Swimming Club was established. Since then, the healthy, useful, and delightful exercise has flourished well'.

Physical prowess and stamina was demonstrated through novice, scratch and handicap swimming races for adults – both members of Brighton Swimming Club and all comers – and boys of different ages. There were also 'grand display[s] of diving and plunging...[and]...swimming under water the greatest distance', demonstrations of swimming in a 'full suit of clothes', floating matches, races for Brighton lifeboat men in their cork jackets ('fettered by the cork jackets the men could not get along very fast, and victory was not the reward of the best swimmer').

More theatrical performances included on Monday 3 August 1868 (the day after the panic on the pier head) 'Captain Camp, the one-legged Swimmer, [who] will prepare and partake of breakfast on the water', and a member of the swimming Club who 'will perform Airs upon the Concertina, and read the Daily Paper whilst lying on the water'. There were frequent performances of events such as walking the greasy pole, (human) duck hunts – with ducks as prizes, Indian Catamaran Canoe Races 'between four Natives', 'the West pier sea horses...[going]...through a sea-circus performance that was most exhilarating', exhibitions of Boyton's life saving suit, and 'foot ball' and polo matches.

Although the swimming matches and aquatic entertainments and sports were dominated by male participants, the prowess of individual women was often proclaimed in the press. In 1875 'two plucky young ladies...fought

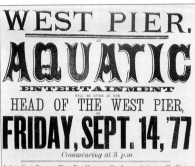

through a rough sea from Shoreham Harbour to the West Pier'. Two years later at the aquatic fête on 19 September 1877, Miss Saigeman's 'graceful swimming and diving were greatly admired by the assembled company, who cheered heartily. The tinge of burlesque which, at the outset, was given to the proceedings by Mr Rowell (who was dressed as an artizan) falling into the water and being rescued by his spouse (Miss Saigemen), set the spectators in an uproar'.

Human ingenuity in and under the water was even brought on to the Pier. In 1889 visitors could pay sixpence for a back seat or one shilling for a front seat to witness 'the model undine', Miss Louie Webb (probably taking her surname from Captain Webb, the first cross Channel swimmer) in 'her unique, scientific, and graceful under-water performance in the glass tank' in one of the Pier kiosks. While submerged in three feet of water Miss Webb performed a variety of feats including eating sponge cake, drinking milk from a bottle, 'opening and closing the eyes', 'attitude of prayer' and sewing and writing.

Late on in the century the pier deck and kiosks became the site for an increasing number of other performances and acts. By 1890 a flea circus included feats such as a 'timber wagon drawn by fleas' and a flea 'duel with steel swords'. In the Edwardian years James Doughty, 'the oldest living actor

and clown', worked the Pier with his performing dogs. The passive and sedate promenade Pier increasingly gave way to spectacle and performance on what was becoming a pleasure pier.

As a speculative venture the new Pier was a success during the first two decades. It was usual for half a million people to pay to visit the Pier in each six month period to the end of August, although numbers were substantially lower in the autumn and winter months. Visitor numbers reached a high point of 845,165 in 1880. Shareholders benefited from the success with, for example, a dividend of 12 per cent being paid in 1876 and 1884, although this was not quite as high as the at least 15 per cent 'safely anticipated' in the 1863 prospectus.

Admission charges to the Pier were the major source of income. Of the Company's total revenue of £3053 for the six months to the end

26 ⟡ PANORAMIC VIEWS OF HOVE FROM THE MINARET AT THE TOP OF A PIER HEAD KIOSK

27 ⟡ THE SPECTACLE OF AN AQUATIC TEA PARTY 1882

28 ⬥ FLEAS ON THE PIER

**29 ⬥ PROFESSOR DOUGHTY, 'THE OLDEST
LIVING ACTOR AND CLOWN', AND HIS
PERFORMING DOGS**

of February 1891, 63 per cent came from pier tolls and 29 per cent from renting space. For August 1893 alone, over 82 per cent of the Company's monthly receipts came from tolls and the sale of programmes. From the mid-1880s, however, the Pier Company profits declined. In 1886 the October half-yearly meeting of the Company recommended a dividend for the year of only 6 per cent, 'considerably less than has been paid in previous years'. The Chairman of the Company, Joseph Ellis, complained about the rival attractions of 'the showmen of the Brighton Corporation' and also announced the need for 'some works for the maintenance of the stability of the pier'. The dividend for shareholders was little better the following year, Mr Ellis bemoaning 'the rivalry...of corporation bands and entertainments with all the assistance of palaces and gardens and public money'. By 1888 the number of people going through the turnstiles had declined to 590,651, the lowest ever annual number of visitors on the Pier.

From the early 1890s an even greater danger than Brighton Corporation threatened the West Pier. Its position as Brighton's most modern and fashionable pier was challenged by the building of the Palace Pier as the replacement for the old and increasingly unstable Chain Pier. ⬥

CHAPTER THREE

THE PLEASURE PIER

'in a holiday mood'

30 ❖ THE COMPLETED WEST PIER IN ITS HEYDAY WITH CONCERT HALL, LANDING STAGES, BATHING STATION AND SAND ARTIST

By the last decade of the century the promenade Pier could not be sustained as a viable enterprise. Beginning in 1891, the building of the larger and modern Palace Pier, designed from the outset to include a massive pavilion for all sorts of entertainment, was a major threat to the West Pier. The Company also had to respond to changing holiday fashions and other sources of competition in resort Brighton. If the West Pier was to survive as a speculative venture it had to stop being first and foremost a promenade pier. It needed to take on a new role, and this required major investment beyond the resources of the existing Pier Company.

On 7 March 1890 a Special General Meeting of the Pier Company's shareholders was held in the Brighton Town Hall and provisional agreement reached to sell the Pier. A new West Pier Company was incorporated by the West Pier

31 ✧ THE PALACE PIER SHORTLY AFTER
COMPLETION IN 1901 SHOWING THE
ORNATE ORIENTAL PIER HEAD PAVILION

Act 1890, with much increased capital: 25,000 £1 shares sold at £10 each. In July 1890 the prospectus for the new Company was issued, authorising a share capital of £100,000 in 10,000 £10 shares and borrowing powers of £25,000. The purpose of the Company was to acquire 'the undertaking and property of the original Brighton West Pier Company, with powers to erect a pavilion on the pier head, and to carry out other extensions and improvements'.

As with the 1866 West Pier Company, the new 1890 Company was essentially a locally and regionally owned speculative business. Seven out of ten shareholders came from Brighton and Hove and another ten per cent from elsewhere in Sussex. Many had held shares in the old Pier Company. The shareholders covered a wide social and occupational array. At one extreme were gentlemen, surgeons, ship owners and army officers, including, for example, Sir Robert Murray of Brunswick Square. Described in the Company records as a Gentleman, he bought 25 shares in 1890 but sold them within four years. At the other extreme were small shopkeepers, masons, widows and laundresses, owning just a few shares and often keeping them for many years. Ellen Shrivell, a laundress living in Temple Street, Brighton, bought ten shares in 1890 and kept them for three decades until she died in 1920.

Following the formation of the new Company, the income-generating potential of the Pier was realised through

32 ✧ THE PAVILION'S INTERIOR BEFORE
THE 1903 CONVERSION INTO A THEATRE

major investment in large new pier buildings and associated works. In 1893 the substructure of the pier head was strengthened and its load bearing potential massively increased. The pier head was widened by 40 feet on both the east and west sides, with much of the original space being transformed and used as the site for a large pavilion. The eastern and western sections of original weather screening were moved to the neck of the Pier, the first steps in giving shelter to people walking to the end of the Pier. South of the new Pavilion, the curved section of the old weather screening was used as part of a new open air bandstand. The Pavilion was enlarged two years later and then, in 1903, converted into a Theatre with seating for over 1000 people. Between 1893 and 1896 a landing stage of mild steel was constructed around three sides of the pier head, allowing for much easier use of the Pier by the expanding steamer excursion business. It was enlarged in 1901. The 1893 reconstruction of the pier head included bathing accommodation for visitors and, although rebuilt several times, bathing facilities continued as a feature of the Pier into the post Second World War period. By 1900 electricity was installed on the Pier. The building of the central Concert Hall, begun in 1914 but delayed by the outbreak of the First World War, was not completed until 1916. By this time, more than a quarter of a century after the formation of the 1890 Company, the Pier was equipped to provide a wide variety of indoor

33 ❖ **THE WEST PIER AFTER THE GREAT STORM OF 4 AND 5 DECEMBER 1896. THE DAMAGE WAS CAUSED BY WRECKAGE FROM THE CHAIN PIER AND BY TIMBER LEFT ON THE BEACH BY BRIGHTON COUNCIL CONTRACTORS**

34 ❖ **REDEVELOPMENT OF THE PIER HEAD LED TO A HUGE INCREASE IN THE NUMBER OF VISITORS. AT THE TURN OF THE CENTURY WOMEN WERE EAGER TO PROTECT THEMSELVES FROM DIRECT EXPOSURE TO THE SUN**

and outdoor entertainment, completing the transformation of the structure from a promenade pier into an all year round pleasure pier.

The first of these changes occurred within sight of Brighton's older and newer piers to the east. The Palace Pier was planned as a replacement for the increasingly decrepit Chain Pier. The Chain Pier itself, by then owned by the Brighton Marine Palace and Pier Company building the new pier, was destroyed in a storm on the 4 and 5 of December 1896. In its death throes it seemed eager to take its old rival, the West Pier, with it. Chain Pier wreckage destroyed a 100-foot section of the West Pier above the beach, stranding a clerk and several waitresses. The columns supporting the western root end kiosk were also damaged and the new bathing rooms swept away. The West Pier Company sued its rival (and Brighton Corporation which had been carrying out beach works using balks of timber which the December storm threw against the Pier) for several thousand pounds in damages.

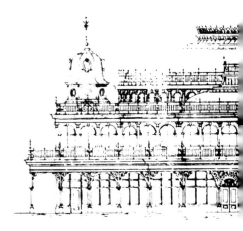

The building of the Palace Pier took a decade, the scheme almost being abandoned on a number of occasions before it was eventually completed in 1901. The Marine Palace and Pier Company faced a series of financial difficulties and a number of legal challenges from the West Pier Company eager to do what it could to hinder or stop the building of the competitor pier. The delay gave the West Pier Company a massive start in the contest to develop a pleasure pier for Brighton. Once the Palace Pier opened, however, the two piers entered a period when they raced neck and neck for the position as Brighton's premier seaside attraction. The West Pier Company turned its pavilion into a theatre in 1903 and within a few years the Palace Pier company followed suit, converting its 1901 pavilion into a theatre in 1910-11. In the same year an elaborate new winter garden building was opened on the Palace Pier. The West Pier Company responded with the central Concert Hall begun four years later in 1914.

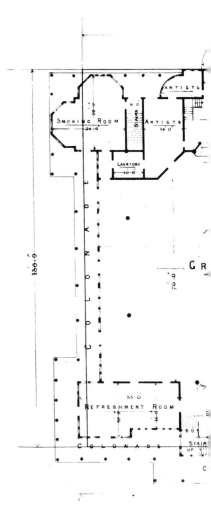

Although Eugenius Birch died in 1884, the family remained involved with the Pier. His nephew, RW Peregrine Birch (1845-96), was the civil engineer in charge of 1890s pier head works. His proposed plans for the new Pavilion, dated 4 February 1891, show a 100-foot wide building, with a veranda encircling the exterior and roofed by an imposing oriental dome, echoing the Royal Pavilion. Inside, the ground floor contained a grand hall with orchestra space at the south

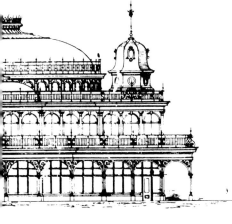

end and entrance lobby, refreshments room and separate ladies tea room to the north. Upstairs the eight-sided balcony floor featured a circular gallery.

This proposal was altered significantly. The Chairman of the Company reported to a shareholders meeting in October 1893 that the directors 'tried hard to get a more ornamental roof, with a dome or pinnacle in the centre, but the (Brighton) Corporation would not give way, and, after considerable delay, they were compelled to adopt the "flattened, dish-cover roof"' which the building now presented'.

The Pavilion that was opened on 19 October 1893 was designed as a flexible space for entertainment with an emphasis on music. As with the Pier's earlier buildings, the framework made it 'almost entirely an iron building. The framing consists of wrought iron girders supported upon upwards of 100 ornamental cast-iron columns'. The building was 125 feet long and 100 feet wide. It was surrounded by a colonnade on all four sides providing shelter and also access to 'rows of shops, forming bazaars' – a novel feature which the Pier Company thought would add to the income generation potential of the new building. In an echo of the promenade pier, the 18-foot wide roof of the colonnade was to be used as 'an extra promenade': 'This magnificent marine terrace, as it virtually is, surrounds the pavilion, giving shelter and shade as desired, in all states of the wind, and it affords magnificent prospects seaward or landward, commanding an unrivalled panoramic view of Brighton front and its environs, from Selsey Bill on the one hand to Beachey Head on the other'.

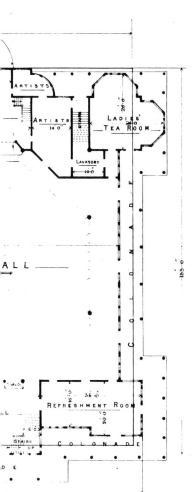

Left

35 AND 36 ⋄ PEREGRINE BIRCH'S ORIGINAL 1891 PROPOSALS FOR THE PIER HEAD PAVILION. THEY WERE SUBSTANTIALLY MODIFIED INCLUDING THE REMOVAL OF THE LARGE ONION DOME

Right

37 ⋄ ARCHITECT'S CROSS SECTION OF THE NEW WEATHER SCREENS ADDED TO THE PIER NECK DURING THE 1890S

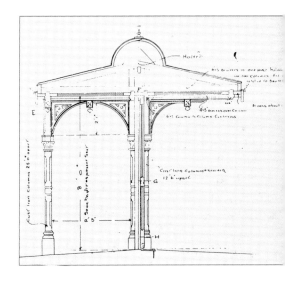

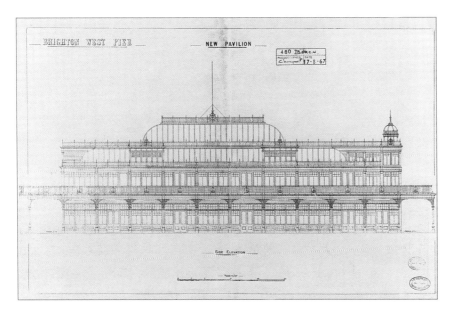

38 ❖ BIRCH'S REVISED 1892 PLANS FOR THE PAVILION AS BUILT

39 ❖ LISTENING TO THE WONDERS OF PETTETT'S WIRELESS SERVICE ON THE PIER HEAD

Inside the building was a foyer, refreshment rooms on the ground and first floors, the Company's offices, a telephone 'for the use of subscribers', a telegraph office, and rooms for artistes. Much the largest space was taken by the 'Hall of entertainments', entered from the foyer through glass doors, and 'fitted by a well appointed stage'. Inside the grand hall, according to the London *Daily Telegraph* correspondent, 'the elegant interior is not lavishly decorated, but the colouring, in two shades of green, relieving white, is pretty and the whole tone of the place very cheerful and bright'. The hall seated between 1200 and 1400 people in the main auditorium (reports varied) and perhaps 300 people in the balcony.

The *Daily Telegraph* acclaimed the building as providing 'Brighton with an establishment which surpasses all its rivals, and may be made to correspond in every desirable detail with the attractive casinos of continental resorts'.

In the first year of the Pavilion's use, music was an important but not dominant focus. Musical entertainments included a diverse range of styles and performers. Many performances included the West Pier band conducted by Mr H S Gates and, in the first few months, the West Pier Choral Union. The local and national press repeated the Company's slogan, 'popular music at popular prices'. There were 'popular ballad concerts' for which 'seats 6d; side seats and balcony 3d; a few numbered front seats, one shilling, may be booked in advance' and in 1894 a series of evening vocal and orchestral Promenade Concerts. There were also evenings of national songs and ballads, Irish music and 'a special Scotch concert'.

The performances of 'Gems from English Light Opera' were typical of the Pavilion's musical light entertainment. On other occasions visitors could hear 'the accomplished Russian vocalist Mdme. Recoschewitz, [who] has been received with every sign of satisfaction at each appearance – she has a voice of great beauty and capacity, and what is more, uses it to splendid

effect'. The Barrington Foote Concert and Operetta Company provided 'a capital programme consisting of no fewer than sixteen vocal and instrumental items'. In a still lighter tone, Mr George Pritchard's musical sketches included 'a humorous description of a musical evening on board ship, where the monotonous fog-horn plays a cruel part in "The Death of Nelson"...and...a realistic vocal imitation of a zither'. The Burgon Opera Recital Company included 'a charming interpretation of selections from Balfe's beautiful opera "The Bohemian Girl"'. Other weeks featured musical entertainments provided by Mr C Emlyn Jones and the Cardiff National Welsh Choir; Miss Edith Hands' Ballard Concert Company; and, the Anglo-Swiss Ladies' Orchestra and Concert Party.

The most successful performers were often retained for additional weeks or else re-engaged in later

40 ⬧ THE PIER SHORTLY AFTER THE COMPLETION OF THE PAVILION

41 ⬧ ARCHITECT'S PERSPECTIVE OF THE PAVILION DRAWN IN 1892

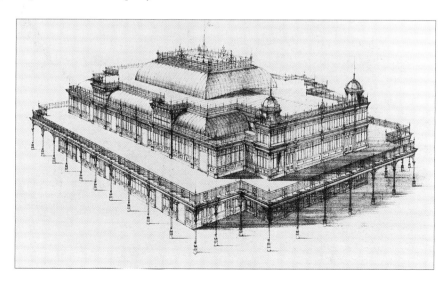

42 ⬩ AN EARLY VIEW OF THE
PLEASURE PIER WITH A STEAMER
AT THE PIER HEAD

months. The latter was true of two acts together on the same bill, the Bandurria Troubadours, in Spanish costume and playing mandolin and guitar, and the Musical Mozarts, 'American musical comedians'. Such performers edged close to variety. One critic was especially impressed by a bird imitator: 'To hear Mrs Albert Barker, the well-known reciter, in "The Birds' Singing Lesson," the wonderful and most melodious imitations of the bob-o'-link, swallow, sparrow, and others, is, however, alone worth a visit'.

As the first year wore on, non-musical acts featured more strongly in the Pavilion's repertoire. Three entertainers to return on a number of occasions

43 ⬩ AN UNUSUAL VIEW OF THE
CROWDED PIER HEAD SHOWING
THE BATHING STATION

were 'that monarch of mimics, Mr. Henry Wardroper'; Mr Fred Evered, 'the popular female impersonator'; and, Mr Victor André, whose 'conjuring and sleight-of-hand tricks are most cleverly done'. One critic at least was not totally convinced by Victor André, describing him as 'dexterous as a conjuror, inventive as an illusionist, fairly good as a ventriloquist'. The press also

criticised 'M. Jean Rollon, "The Scientific Athlete", a self-possessed French-man of more than ordinary proportions, who, having introduced himself in a song describing the virtues of a quack medicine, proceeded to give practical evidence of its wonderful effect on him in a series of "strong-man" acrobatic feats'. In contrast there were excellent reviews of Mazeppa, 'the wonderfully intelligent talking and calculating horse': 'should you ask her to do an impossible thing – such as take 4 from 2 – she will shake her head with vigour, just to show how ridiculous you are making yourself'.

Hotel Metropole, Brighton

Copyright

44 ❖ SWIMMERS, RAFTS AND DINGHIES OFF THE BATHING STATION

The success of Mr Horace G Banks' dioramic views of the United States, 'certainly the best Brighton has ever seen', with the pictures being 'thrown on a sheet across the stage', led to the engagement of Professor Malden with fine photographic and dioramic slides. The Professor's shows included one taking 'his audiences in imagination for tours...through "Our Glorious Colonies"'.

The new Pavilion was well-patronised. Occasionally, however, the weather intervened. One critic noted that 'the audience present on Tuesday night was a somewhat scanty one, the numbers being evidently affected by the continuous downpour of rain, under which circumstances the Pier is bound to suffer'. The 1893 Christmas entertainment, performed by Mrs Albert Barker, was in part aimed at children: 'the programme is composed of Christmas stories, fairy tales, and short recitations'. Bad weather again intruded since 'at the outset the roaring of the sea and the whistling of the wind made it difficult for her voice to be heard, so she made the request to the audience to draw more closely to the platform'.

The Pier Company was eager to push at the boundaries of how the Pavilion could be used. One innovation at the end of August 1894 was the Brighton Pet Dog Show with £600 in prizes – 'the first occasion on which a dog show has been held on the broad briny'. There was also a temporary

Art Gallery at the north end of the Pavilion balcony , the 'fifty valuable old paintings' which were for sale included works by Rubens, Gainsborough and Dürer. Late on in 1894 the Pier Company organised 'Society Socials', with the 'handsome interior of the Pavilion...transformed out of all resemblance to a set concert room...with a refined entertainment...much as might be given in a first-class drawing room.... It is said that more stylish people and smarter toilettes put in an appearance there than anywhere else in Brighton, not even excepting "Prayer-Book Parade"' (on the Hove seafront lawns on Sunday mornings after church).

Brighton Council had reserved for itself the controlling power to say whether dancing could take place in the Pavilion. In May 1894 there was a heated Council discussion about the issue, with a small minority of Councillors believing the Pier was potentially unsafe and unstable. The Company, however, received the permission it required and there was a grand ball in July 1894 with dancing on a platform erected in the middle of the hall. The Company's and Council's faith in the structure was rewarded since 'although a strong wind was blowing the floor kept "quite steady"'.

The great variety of entertainment provided during the Pavilion's first year of use included few plays. Those that were performed were usually insubstantial. They included the Redgrave Sketch Combination 'appearing

45 ◇

46 ◇

47 ◇ PROFESSOR REDDISH DIVING
FROM THE PIER HEAD

in the farcical sketch *The Second Mrs Chester*' and another troop performing the 'once well-known farce, *Two in the Morning* .... the performance
showed unmistakable signs of inadequate rehearsal, a particularly unfor-
tunate failing for a piece of this class'. It was not until the turn of the century
that plays came to dominate the repertoire.

The Pavilion – 'this popular place of amusement' – was the jewel in
the West Pier crown. But the enlarged pier head allowed the Company to
develop the West Pier in a number of other ways. In particular, the sea itself
was exploited through the development of public swimming, displays of
professional diving and aquatic entertainments, and the extension of the
paddle steamer excursion business.

A press report in May 1893 commented on 'the bathing facilities which
are afforded at the head of the Pier from which a dip in the briny can be
indulged in daily from six till eleven a.m.' and 10,300 visitors used the new
bathing rooms in the six months to the end of August. In the following year
the bathing season started on Thursday 9 May. The Company was keen to
advertise the new facilities on the east side of the pier head: 'A long range of
bathing-rooms, fitted internally with every convenience, has been newly erected,
with special rooms for members of clubs'. Perhaps in response to changes in
public taste or to make the bathing experience less exclusive, at the same time
the Company also announced that 'in right appreciation of public feeling it
has been decided that in the future persons bathing after nine o'clock shall
wear a becoming bathing costume'. Although the bathing station was never a
significant feature of the Pier Company's income, it was expressive of the pier
experience particularly during the first half of the twentieth century.

The redeveloped pier head was also used for other sea-based entertainments including some still involving Brighton Swimming Club, evening
Venetian Fêtes and displays of 'aquatic fireworks by Brock'. In 1894 the
West Pier Company and Brighton Swimming Club were negotiating a detailed
agreement. The Company's proposal was to provide 'your Club with a room
adjacent to the present new bathing-rooms...fitted with shower or douche
appliances, urinal and chair; they will also provide a way down underneath
the present landing-stage together with diving board for bathing purposes'.
In return the Club would 'give free of charge to the Company not less than

48 ✧

49 ✧

50 ✧ THE FAMOUS WEST PIER DIVERS

51 ❖

52 ❖

53 ❖

16 public exhibitions of swimming and polo-matches' during the season. Perhaps because sea swimming became more popular as a public activity and less of a spectacle, the Swimming Club provided fewer exhibitions and aquatic entertainments, concentrating instead on polo. The arrangement between Club and Company continued into the first few years of the new century – there was a series of water polo matches illuminated 'by limelight' on Monday evenings during the summer of 1903 – but then petered out.

By the 1920s the 'bay of the West Pier', within the landing stages, was used as the venue for the aquatic sports element of the Brighton Carnival – inspired by the Nice Carnival – held in early summer. As part of the 1923 Carnival, the pier head was used for the Ladies' Bathing Costume Pageant and Parade with both trade and private entries. The entries included Marjory Taylor dressed as a mermaid and representing Bon Marche of Western Road and Muriel Sutherland, representing Leeson and Vokins of North Street, who wore a pale cream costume, trimmed with oriental colours, with a royal blue cape.

The Pier was also used by a new breed of professional marine entertainers and, in particular, divers. Echoing the swimming displays of the earlier promenade pier, professional diving was an aquatic entertainment that combined demonstrations of physical prowess and skill with elements of theatre. Two noted early West Pier divers were Professor Reddish and Professor Cyril. Apart from their adopted academic titles both had a theatrical approach to their work. Professor Cyril (real name Albert Huggins Heppell), 'the great exponent of High, Swedish and Fancy Diving', made the ultimate spectacular sacrifice during his 'sensational bicycle dive' on 27 May 1912. He was killed when, attempting his frequently accomplished feat, he 'had a side-slip and was thrown heavily on to the deck of the pier, fracturing his skull'.

Other West Pier divers – both men and women – used diving boards, some towering 80 feet into the sky, on the eastern side of the new landing stages and facing into the bay of the Pier. Spectators, watching the performance from both the landing stages and the edge of the pier proper, were encouraged to contribute to collections for the divers. Particularly well known were Walter Tong, Zoe Brigden and Gladys Powsey. Although professionals, they had mostly come up through the ranks of amateur clubs. Tong, born in Bolton in 1892, and a member of Bolton Swimming Club for eight years, was also described as a 'high and fancy diver and ornamental swimmer' and 'professional diver and life-saving champion'. At one stage assisted by Miss May Victoria, 'a good diver and swimmer, her displays attracting much attention', immediately before the First World War Tong's own special feats included his famous 'Moleberg' and 50-foot dives.

Zoe Brigden, from a local Brighton family, was the town's amateur swimming champion for almost a decade until she turned professional in 1913. She became a diver after a shoulder injury forced her to quit professional swimming. For two years she worked on the Pier with Walter Tong and then for a further seven years, until retiring in 1925, she performed on the West Pier alone. Included in her act was the 'wooden soldier' dive where with arms at her sides she plunged head first into the sea. She made a strong impression on one young visitor to the Pier, Mavis Ward, who talking in 1997 remembers 'There was one woman, who had a megaphone who used to say "come and see me dive from the bay at the end of the pier". There was a rumour went round that she had swallowed an octopus, and that it was eating her inside...She wore a dressing gown, while she was going up and down the pier, a towelling thing'. Gladys Powsey, often wearing a costume emblazoned with 'Bovril' across the chest, included in her act an imitation of a seal swimming, diving and calling out. Mr John Moss remembers an exhibition diver, Roy Brooks, calling himself 'Aquamaniac', performing 'very spectacular and beautifully done' dives at the pier head in the summer of 1939.

Although used for professional diving and quickly becoming a popular venue for fishing, the major purpose of the new landing stages was for the steamer excursion business – loading and unloading passengers taking a pleasure trip on the sea. Pleasure steamers were travelling and unstable extensions of seaside piers. On 18 July 1894 among the vessels using the West Pier were the *Windsor Castle* carrying 360 passengers from Bournemouth, the *Conqueror* from Hastings with 167 passengers, the *Princess May* on her return trip from Worthing, and the *Brighton* 'with short-trip passengers'. The *Brighton* was effectively the Pier's own steamer, carrying 1,400 people on short trips on Easter Monday, 1893. The *Princess May*, a frequent visitor to the West Pier, was built on the Clyde and finished in 1893. She carried 400 passengers on her two decks and was 'fitted up in a luxurious style'. In

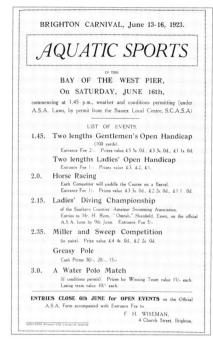

BRIGHTON CARNIVAL, June 13-16, 1923.

AQUATIC SPORTS

IN THE
BAY OF THE WEST PIER,
On SATURDAY, JUNE 16th,
commencing at 1.45 p.m., weather and conditions permitting (under A.S.A. Laws, by permit from the Sussex Local Centre, S.C.A.S.A)

LIST OF EVENTS.

1.45. **Two lengths Gentlemen's Open Handicap**
(100 yards).
Entrance Fee 2/-. Prizes value £5 5s. 0d., £3 3s. 0d., £1 1s. 0d.
Two lengths Ladies' Open Handicap
Entrance Fee 1/-. Prizes value £3, £2, £1.

2.0. **Horse Racing**
Each Competitor will paddle the Course on a Barrel.
Entrance Fee 1/-. Prizes value £3 3s. 0d., £2 2s. 0d., £1 1s. 0d.

2.15. **Ladies' Diving Championship**
of the Southern Counties' Amateur Swimming Association.
Entries to Mr. H. Rees, "Omrah," Shenfield, Essex, on the official A.S.A. form by 9th June. Entrance Fee 5/-.

2.35. **Miller and Sweep Competition**
(in pairs). Prize value £4 4s. 0d., £2 2s. 0d.
Greasy Pole
Cash Prizes 30/-, 20/-, 15/-.

3.0. **A Water Polo Match**
(if conditions permit). Prizes for Winning Team value 15/- each.
Losing team 10/- each.

ENTRIES CLOSE 6th JUNE for OPEN EVENTS on the Official A.S.A. Form accompanied with Entrance Fee to
F. H. WISEMAN,
4 Church Street, Brighton.

54

55 ◇ THE WEST SIDE OF THE LANDING STAGES WITH A FAMOUS WEST PIER PLEASURE STEAMER, THE BRIGHTON QUEEN

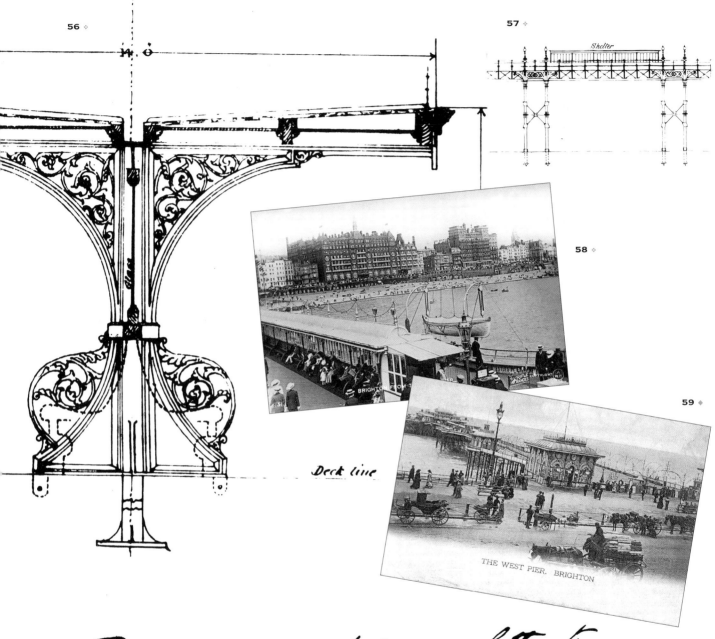

56

57

Shelter

58

59

Deck line

THE WEST PIER. BRIGHTON

*Tracing referred to in my letter to
Mr May of this date.*

4th Feb 1891

*R W Peregrine Birch
Engineer*

60

the dining saloon the walls were of 'American walnut with bird's eye maple panels. The sofas and settees are upholstered in dark blue velvet pile, and the floor is laid with Brussels carpet'.

During the following decades many paddle steamers – including the *Brighton Belle, Brighton Queen, Glen Gower, Glen Rosa, Albion, Ravenswood, Devonia* and *Waverley* – made the West Pier a regular port of call, sometimes also picking up passengers from the Palace Pier before heading for other Sussex resorts or venturing on longer trips to the Isle of Wight or across the Channel to Boulogne or Dieppe.

Shortly after the Pavilion opened, the Company set about re-decking the rest of the Pier and, where possible, finding new uses for the smaller and older ornamental kiosks. One novelty, starting in Easter 1894, was a display of ants. One of the kiosks 'has been admirably fitted up for an exhibition of these curious creatures .... a complete nest of the great hill ant, occupying a glass case in the centre of the kiosk'. Although providing an 'interesting glimpse into the wonders of ant life', the exhibition did not last long. The Company was keen to innovate in other ways, and experiments included a military tattoo, open-air demonstrations of radio broadcasting listened to by packed audiences on the pier head, and a cinema between March and August 1913.

The redevelopment of the pier head had a huge impact on the Pier's popularity. Admission numbers soared, from 623,000 in 1892/93 (the year end being the last day of February) to 1,065.00 the following year. Reporting to his shareholders in April 1894, just six months after the Pavilion opened, Frederick Banister as Chairman of the Company was eager to announce 'a very considerable increase in the Receipts over the corresponding period of last year. This is in a great measure due to the fact that the Pavilion has proved to be most suitable for the purposes for which it was erected. The Entertainments given therein (as well as the rentals from the shops attached thereto) now form an important addition to the revenue of the Company'. By the end of the century, in both 1898 and 1899, the new Company paid a dividend of 9 per cent to its shareholders.

However, within a decade the Pier Company concluded that rather than a pavilion with flexible space, it wanted a permanent theatre. In 1903, just two years after the Palace Pier Company opened its own pier head pavilion with

61 ✧

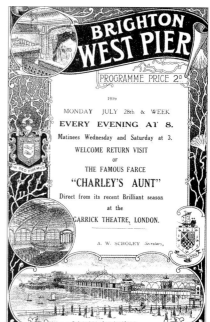

62 ✧

63 ✠ THE AUDITORIUM AND STAGE OF THE THEATRE. THE 1903 CONVERSION INCLUDED AN EXTENSION OF THE BALCONY AND THE INCLUSION OF A SLOPING FLOOR

a concert hall and dining, smoking and reading rooms, major conversion works took place on the West Pier Pavilion. These included extending the balcony area, sloping the previously level floor of the auditorium to improve the view of the stage, and installing permanent seats. The building was renamed the West Pier Theatre. The Theatre contained 1076 seats: 318 in the stalls (subsequently reduced to 298), 167 in the main balcony, 158 at the balcony sides, 292 in the pit stalls and another 12 'chairs in corners', and 129 in the pit. The stage opening was 28 feet wide, 24 feet high with a depth of 23 feet.

For the first three decades of the century the theatre was in use all the year round. The majority of shows were provided by touring or London companies who received a share of the box office receipts ranging from 45 to 75 per cent, although 55 to 65 per cent was typical. In return, the company using the Theatre agreed to a number of rules and regulations, the most important being to 'provide and pay a full, efficient and capable Company for the adequate representation of the play or entertainment'. Other rules required the touring company to provide 'All Perishable Properties, such as Plates to break, Eatables, Drinkables, Fire-arms (sure fire), Gunpowder, Cartridges, Lightning Paper, Cigars, Cigarettes, etc.', and gave the West Pier Company 'the right to object to any Song, Dance, Speech, Look, Posture, Dialogue, "Business," or Costume which in their opinion is indecorous, improper, or unsuited for representation'.

In the first few years of the century one of the most popular companies, making an annual visit for a month, was 'The Mohawk Moore and Burgess Minstrels'. In July 1903, with a 'splendid choir and orchestra', they featured 'the favourite vocalists' and 'the old favourite comedians', the latter including Harry Hunter also known as 'the Centre-Mental Man'. To attract repeat visits by the audience, their programme was 'entirely changed each week' with different days having special 'Plantation', Irish, 'Scotch' or operatic programmes.

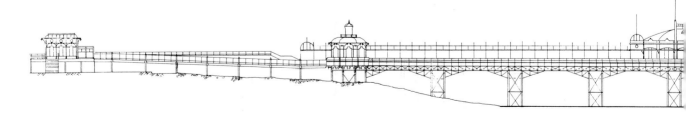

On Sundays there were 'Grand Sacred Concerts' with 'oratorio selections and gems of sacred songs' and 'the Minstrels appearing with White Faces'.

The minstrel fashion soon faded. In the following decades the Theatre carried an amazing array of different plays and stage entertainments from Shakespeare and 'Russian Ballet', through romances, comedies and thrillers, to opera, musicals and the occasional concert party. Most shows and companies changed each week until the 1930s. Exceptionally in one week during April 1908 a company performed five different Shakespearean plays including *As You Like It* and *Romeo and Juliet*. More challenging for the audience was the week of Ibsen in December 1908, with performances of *The Master Builder*, *A Doll's House* and *Hedda Gabler*.

The most popular shows returned year after year. Examples include *The Ghost Train*, *A Little Bit of Fluff*, *Pygmalion*, *Charlie's Aunt*, *A Temporary Gentleman*, *Daddalums*, *Too Young To Marry*, *The Black Spider*, *The Man Who Changed His Name*, *No, No, Nanette* and *Dangerous Corner*. The most successful week of entertainment, grossing the largest box office receipts, and at the peak of the Pier's popularity, was the week ending 23 August 1919. J A E Malone's Company presented two of the 'greatest musical comedy successes' *The Merry Widow* and *Gipsy Love*, taking total receipts for the week of £731.9.8.

The Ghost Train returned to the West Pier on a number of occasions. Written by Arnold Ridley (later famed as Private Godfrey in *Dad's Army*) it achieved its greatest financial success in the week ending 10 September 1927, with box office receipts of £718.11.1. For *The Ghost Train* a good seat in the orchestra stalls cost 3/6d, a ticket for the balcony stalls (presumably with a miserable view) was 6d. The stars of the thriller were H Charles Carew playing Teddy Deakin and Ethel Warwick as Julia Price. Miss Warwick wore a 'Rue de la Paix' gown supplied by Madam Ada of South Molton Street, W.1. Cigarettes used in the performance were supplied by Abdulla.

64 ❖

65 ❖

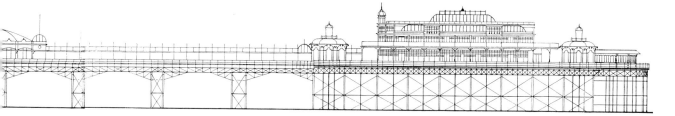

In May 1924 Mrs Patrick Campbell appeared in *The Thirteenth Chair* and *The Second Mrs Tanqueray*, this being described in the notes of one critic as 'a somewhat silly play. Mrs P C exceedingly fat and not too pleasing face. A very full house'. Brighton's own famous comedian, Max Miller, was not a frequent performer on the Pier. Billed as 'the Cheeky Chappie', he did star in two performances of a financially rather unsuccessful concert on the afternoon and evening of Sunday 15 June 1930.

Of the hundreds of performers who appeared on the West Pier during the four decades before the Second World War most are now lost in the mists of British entertainment history. The more famous included Ellen Terry, Edith Evans, Fred Karno, Rex Harrison, Ralph Richardson, Max Jaffa, Cicely Courtneidge, Jean Anderson and Robert Morley. Jean Anderson, talking in 1997, recalls working in the Theatre in 1929: 'There was something about the walk up the Pier at night and feeling you were part of the fun. The West Pier was more up market than the Palace Pier, it was a quieter pier. The Concert Hall had an orchestra nearly every day. The theatre was intimate, whereas the Palace Pier was more like a variety hall. We used to go swimming off the steps at the end of the Pier, off the landing stage, wonderfully refreshing after a matinee and before the evening performance'.

66 ✦ THE FULLY DEVELOPED PIER WITH 1866 KIOSKS, 1893 PAVILION AND CONCERT HALL COMPLETED IN 1916

The Theatre was also used occasionally by local amateur companies and dancing schools and for charity performances in aid of local good causes such as hospitals. Between 1920 and 1922 and again in 1933, the Theatre hosted a number of productions by Brighton and Hove Operatic Society including *Merrie England*, *The Yeoman of the Guard* and *The Mikado*. Mavis Ward, recollects: 'My father was on the committee of the Operatic Society, and they rented the theatre for a week, and they had the takings but also had to pay for the theatre...[the] seats were red, in the twenties, and it was sixpence for a seat, but you had to lean right over the top to see. Red and goldish. Dear little Theatre, very friendly'. Later, in the early 1930s, she ran a stage school: 'we used to do our shows, just for matinees, one performance for the children, and we hired the Theatre, mainly dancing in those days. The Pier was very well looked after. It was quite fashionable to go on the Pier. Underneath the stage there was the sea, and at the side of the stage where the boards had gone a bit, the stagehands used to sit there and fish through the holes, from inside the Theatre, and occasionally they would catch something'.

The Theatre was well known for its Christmas pantomimes and plays. One of the first was the now obscure *The Yellow Dwarf* performed by the Gus Hart Company from 24 December 1898 until 28 January 1899. In the first decade of the century the West Pier's own company performed both traditional pantomimes such as *Dick Whittington* and *Cinderella* and Christmas plays including *Cherry Girl* and *Bluebell in Fairyland*. Few were performed in the dozen years to the 1923-24 season when the 'ever-delightful' *Bluebell in Fairyland*, by Sir Seymour Hicks, was dusted off. In later years the varied diet ranged from *Mother Hubbard* (1925-26) and *Goody Two Shoes* (1926-27) to *Babes in the Wood* (1935-36). *The Forty Thieves* was the final West Pier pantomime, running for two weeks in the 1938-39 season.

The success of the Theatre, and the opening of the Palace Pier's central winter gardens in 1910, led the Pier Company in 1914 to start building a Concert Hall, for musical performances and other events. The 1877 covered bandstand was demolished, the central width of the Pier extended by 14 feet, and a low eight-sided oval Concert Hall was built around a skeleton of iron arches. The structure had a curving roof and low turrets, a 'broad projecting cornice...which makes for a sheltered walk all around the building', and the exterior was decorated with 'Brighton dolphins on shields, set off with heavy festoons. At due intervals on the parapet of the roof arise graceful urns...[which]...suggest champagne rather than ashes'.

The interior of the building was unbroken by pillars or balconies, the sweep of the iron roof trusses resembling 'the delicate fan lines of a Late Gothic roof'. At the time of the opening the press reported that the Hall

67 ⊹ THE WEST PIER'S GREAT RIVAL THE PALACE PIER, WITH THE CENTRAL WINTER GARDEN OPENED IN 1910

PALACE PIER, BRIGHTON.

68 ✧ THE WEST PIER ORCHESTRA
IN THE CONCERT HALL 1923. THE
CONDUCTOR WAS FRANK GOMEZ
WHO SUCCEEDED LYELL TAYLOR

69 ✧ OUTSIDE THE CONCERT HALL ON
A SUNNY WEEKEND IN THE MID-1920S

seated up to 1400 people, although the actual number was probably much smaller. The building was designed for a variety of uses; the floor could be cleared and the space used as a ballroom or for roller skating. Inside 'the place seems all windows', the floor was in different tints of red and the white walls had 'panels above and below the chief range of windows with graceful stencilled designs in soft colourings...[and a]...moulded cornice picked out in gold'. This unique building, designed by Clayton and Black and engineered by Noel Ridley, was described at the time as 'a comely, well proportioned structure of a certain individuality of design' and 'architecture in a holiday mood'.

The new hall – 'assured of becoming one of the most popular of the West Pier's many attractions' – was opened on Thursday 20 April 1916. The opening performance by the King's Royal Rifles silver band – 'wounded soldiers or men invalided out of the Army' – had vocal support from Madame Edith Welling and Corporal Sinclair-Coles. The programme included the Raymond overture, a selection from *Faust*, *Finlandia*, *A Southern Wedding*, *Parisian Sketches* and *Michigan*. Madame Welling sang *Land of Hope and Glory* and *Love's Garden of Roses*, while Corporal Sinclair-Cole followed with *I Hear You Calling Me*, *Leonore* and *Songs of Araby*.

By November the West Pier's own orchestra was playing in the Concert Hall. From 1918 until 1921 it was under the direction of Lyell Taylor, an eccentric and autocratic conductor who 'specialised mainly in high-class music'. If people arrived late he 'would break out with some such remark as "Tell those people to sit down and not interrupt the performance"'. The leader of the West Pier Orchestra was Albert Ketelby, the composer of *In a Monastery Garden*. Some music making during the 1920s included the performance of 'serious' modern music. Local music critics were not always sure what to make of such work. On the afternoon of 13 November 1925 Paul Belinfante and four 'thoroughly competent musicians' gave a recital of chamber music. 'It was not everybody's music. But it was music that the student gets but rare opportunity of hearing, and it was presented in a thoroughly competent and musicianly way'. For one reviewer, the performance of the Quartet in G minor by Vaughan Williams was 'uncompromisingly modern, with a good deal that sounds like experimenting in other than the commonly accepted scales .... One may as well admit frankly that, even were this a great work, it would need a tremendous amount of ear training to appreciate its greatness. The idiom is harsh to the unaccustomed ear. Indeed, it often sounds merely grotesque'.

The completion of the Concert Hall in 1916 marked the end of the quarter of a century evolution of the West Pier from a promenade into a pleasure pier. This transformation was reflected in the sources of the Pier Company's income. Whereas the old promenade pier received over 60 per cent of its income from admission tolls, for the month of August 1920, 34 per cent of the Company's receipts came from tolls and associated ticket sales for entrance to the Pier, 43 per cent from Theatre and Concert Hall income, and the remaining 23 per cent of revenue from other activities including the bathing station, aquatic entertainments, pier head fishing, automatic machines, rentals and even the charges for using the West Pier lavatories.

As the pleasure pier developed so visitor numbers evolved. During the two decades following the redevelopment of the pier head in the early 1890s, annual visitor numbers kept above the million, sometimes substantially so, and in 1910/11 almost one and a half million people paid to go through the Pier's turnstiles. The number of visitors declined with the start of the First World War, reaching a low point of 894,000 in 1915/16. But in the half a decade following the opening of the Concert Hall in 1916 the West Pier reached its zenith of success and popularity. There were over two million admissions in 1918/19 and in the following year the Pier achieved its highest ever recorded figure of 2,074,000 paying visitors. The Pier was well attuned to holiday fashions and tastes and offered a vast range of open air and indoor leisure attractions. ❧

70 ✦ LYELL TAYLOR THE ECCENTRIC CONDUCTOR OF THE WEST PIER ORCHESTRA BETWEEN 1918-21

71 ✦

CHAPTER FOUR

THE FUNFAIR PIER

'all the fun of the fair'

72 ✧

73 ✧

74 ✧ THE PIER'S SKETCH ARTIST IN THE 1960S

The success of the pleasure pier did not last. From the early 1920s the Pier began a relatively rapid and bumpy descent from the summit of achievement just after the First World War. From over two million visitors in 1919/20 admissions fell to under 1,290,000 a decade later. The decline continued during the 1930s and by 1938/39 visitor numbers were less than 760,000. Within 20 years the Pier lost almost two-thirds of its visitors. Why did they leave and where did they go?

Between the wars holiday-making became increasingly self-centred and, especially out-of-doors, active. Rather than being the relatively passive audience for professional performers, ever more holiday-makers made their own holidays in a variety of ways. There was an increasing enchantment with the pleasures of the sun and sea and, ideally, sand. The West Pier not only faced the rivalry of the Palace Pier, but also the challenge of new attractions ranging from cinemas and sports facilities to open air lidos and swimming pools. Brighton as a resort was also changing and, despite advertising campaigns stressing style, fashion and high quality, it became more downmarket perhaps by default rather than intent. The town experienced intense competition from newer rivals such as Bournemouth and the expanding West country seaside resorts.

The decline of the pleasure pier was experienced in a number of ways. By 1929 Harold Clunn, a commentator on seaside resorts, noted the Pier's decreasing popularity and rapid changes in some of its entertainments during the 1920s, adding that 'the deck of the pier is in much need of repair'. At the front line in trying to stem the decline of visitor numbers was A W Scholey, the Secretary to the Company and Entertainment Manager, who begun work on the Pier, as a cashier, in 1897 and continued until 1952.

In the Concert Hall the serious music of the type directed by Lyell Taylor became less popular in the 1920s. Instead the building became a venue for occasional concert parties, military bands and dance bands and light orchestras. Military bands most often performed in the summer. They included those of the Cheshire Regiment, the Royal Sussex Regiment, the Third Carabiniers, the Second Battalion East Lancashire Regiment, the East Yorkshire Regiment, the Royal Horse Guards and the Royal Tank Corps. The Concert Hall's 11-week 1935 summer season was dominated by military bands and orchestras, the one eccentricity being the 'riot of colour and melody' provided by Petulengro and his Gipsy Hussars. Dance bands and light orchestras, such as Bobbie Hind and his Band, the Long Island Band and Leslie Gann's West Pier Bijou Orchestra (much reduced in both size and ambition in comparison with Lyell Taylor's Orchestra) featured more in the winter months.

Nick Nissen, a musician in the Jan Ralfini orchestra for several summer seasons, remembers the Concert Hall in the late 1930s: 'We went there in

75 ⊹ RELAXING ON THE LANDING STAGES, MID-1930S

1938, fairly large orchestra. Geoff Love was in the orchestra with us before he had a band of his own. I played the violin. Jan Ralfini was well known in those days. We went right through until the beginning of the war. We used to love it there because there was a nice atmosphere in the Concert Hall. It had a bandstand in the middle, it wasn't a big building. The audiences were marvellous. They were mostly middle-aged and elderly, but you would get young ones as well. We played all kinds of popular music, musical comedy, classical, all kinds, very versatile orchestra. The West Pier was always a favourite'.

The Pier's declining popularity had consequences for the Theatre. During the 1930s it was dark for a part of most winters; in 1932 it closed from mid-October until Boxing Day, and in 1935 from mid-January until the Easter re-opening on 20 April. As audiences and box office receipts fell away – in many weeks less than £100 was taken – the Theatre became less attractive to touring companies, especially ones with star performers. Instead, the Pier Company tried to use the Theatre in other ways. One innovation in October and November 1933, not repeated in later years, was a lecture series. Topics ranged from the popular 'Sweeping through Germany with Hitler's Army', given by Captain H Plunkett-Wood (£14.18.8 receipts) to the less successful 'Our Weather and the Beauty of the Skies' by D C Rutherfurd (receipts of £3.10.10).

Concert parties also became a regular part of the Theatre's summer season during the 1930s. Previously they had rarely performed on the Pier, instead being part of Brighton sea front al fresco entertainment. Even the famous and long established Jack Sheppard's Entertainers occasionally moved from their regular seafront pitch opposite the Metropole Hotel on to the Pier itself, especially at Bank Holiday weekends.

In 1935 the 'Jubilee Follies' and 'Cecil's Celebrity Concerts' performed alternative weeks in April and May and the 'West Pier Vanities' ran from June to early August. 'Follies' was made up of a mixture of singing, dancing and comedy acts – in early May it included June and Jerrome with 'their comedy offering'; Edna Cecil, 'the Queen of Melody' playing selections on her violin; Michael Ivan 'The Cossack Tenor'; and the Jubilee Belles 'all merry and bright...with their peppy stepping'. 'West Pier Vanities – The-Up-To-The-Minute-Revue' included over 20 different items. Most concert parties on the Pier were not a great financial success, with Vanities taking receipts of only £45.2.2. in the week ending 27 July 1935 at the height of the summer season.

76 ◈ BETTY RICHARDS AND
OTHER MEMBERS OF THE CAST OF
'NO, NO, NANETTE' SEPTEMBER 1935

Plays and musicals returned to the theatre in the late summer of 1935, attracting larger audiences and greater box office receipts; the most successful show being the musical comedy *No, No, Nanette* in the first week of September with gross receipts of £435.16.3.

Despite the pleasure pier crisis the Pier Company did not, as it had done three or four decades before, change the basic layout and structure of the Pier. There were no substantial new buildings and the Pier was not, as it might have been, made larger or longer. Instead, there were essentially minor additions and changes to the fabric of the Pier, including a new raised entrance at the shore end in 1932 and, three years later, a new bathing station and sun terrace on the eastern landing stage.

The sun terrace and bathing station which opened in August 1935 were the Pier Company's response to the challenge posed by holiday-makers wanting a suntan and to play in water. Single bathing tickets, including admission to the Pier, were 6d. Bathing was mixed (previously Brighton's bathing beaches had been segregated by gender) and 'boat and experienced men [were] always in attendance'. The bathing station was open from 9 am to 1 pm, although the statement 'bathing in costume after 9 am' in the Pier's regulations and terms of admission suggests nude swimming still took place in the early morning.

Some local people have fond memories of swimming from the West Pier between the wars. Mr John Moss recalls the 'marvellous sun terrace and bathing station' in 1935: 'it was marvellous because it meant that people who liked to swim could swim in deep water away from all the crowds without having to hop across the shingle to do it. It was a great place'. By the late 1930s, however, the new facilities were rather poorly patronised by just six or seven thousand people a year. More attractive to many holiday-makers were the delights of open air pools and lidos built in Brighton (and most other seaside towns) during the inter-war years. The municipal Black Rock Swimming Pool opened in 1936 and Saltdean Lido, a private venture with modernist architecture, a year later.

77 ❖ JACK SHEPPARD'S CONCERT PARTY WHICH OCCASIONALLY PERFORMED ON THE PIER DURING THE 1930S

Just as lidos had the added attraction of sunbathing terraces, so by the late 1930s the West Pier advertised its 'sun terraces and sunshine shelters' – a radical change from what the original Victorian promenaders had wanted and expected of the Pier. After the Second World War the quest for the pleasures of sun and sea, combined with rising living standards and cheap air travel, lured holiday-makers to warmer and sunnier overseas holiday destinations. In turn, this exodus was to have a savage impact on most English seaside resorts and piers.

The most important strategy adopted by the Pier Company to entice the lost visitors back on to the Pier was to develop a range of funfair attractions and new amusements. Automatic machines had been a feature of the Pier's entertainments since the early years of the century, generating a significant amount of income – £254 in August 1906 or seven per cent of the

total monthly receipts. Between the wars, however, the Pier Company introduced more mechanical games and amusements. An amusement called Skee
Ball was introduced in 1923. From April 1927 part of the broad root end of
the pier was given over to an 'auto-motor track', which Harold Clunn described
disparagingly as a 'toy motor track, which is anything but an ornament to the
pier .... the writer sincerely hopes that another change of fashion may soon
lead to this disfigurement being replaced by something more pleasing to the
eye'. A Mirror Maze opened in May 1928. The introduction of automatic
gaming machines got the Pier Company into trouble with the Brighton police
when, in January 1929, the Company was charged with unlawful gaming
using a machine called the Domino. By 1937 the Pier featured a large amusement arcade under the reconstructed root end of the Pier and new attractions
including Flash O Ball, Auto Golf and a Phono Disk.

The inter-war character of the Pier is also shown by the businesses
renting space. Throughout the period Findlater Mackie Limited had a lease

78 ❖ **AN EARLY SIGN OF THE FUNFAIR
PIER, THE MINIATURE RACE TRACK WAS
OPENED IN 1927**

with the Pier Company, for use of all the bars and kiosks selling refreshments, at £1000 per annum or 15 per cent of gross receipts. During the 1920s Maynards Limited, well-known confectioners with a sweet factory in Hove, rented the north west kiosk for £100 per year, the Pier entrance shop for £120, and the Concert Hall eastern pay box for £30. Some firms hired advertising space, including Jaeger Limited of London paying 18 guineas a year for an illuminated sign on the windows over the toll houses. The smaller Pavilion shops, selling the like of pictures and silhouettes or fishing tackle, were leased for between £13 and £45 per annum. Smaller amounts were charged for use of outside space. J E Hackman paid 10 shillings a week for using his jockey scales on the Pier deck, while from the 1920s to 1940 Harold Stoner paid one shilling a week to work as a sand artist on the beach at the east side of the Pier. In the late 1930s space for walking a camera on the balustrade and side of the Pier entrance was £30 per year and an artist's pitch was 10 shillings a week. Between 1931 and 1933 General Exhibits Limited paid the greater of £400 per year or 20 per cent of gross receipts to show the Hugh Tussaud Waxworks. In 1933 Nancy Walker, also known as Madame Stellar, paid £84 for her Palmistry Studio. During the 1930s leases were also arranged for the shooting gallery, the speedboat concession, Auto Golf Ltd, amusement arcades, candy floss stalls and sketch portraits.

The Palace Pier to the east took to the funfair business more quickly than the West Pier. Advertising itself as 'the finest pier in the world', by the end of the 1930s it not only had Jimmy Hunter's Brighton Follies playing in the Theatre in the summer season but also open-air dancing, a 'palace of fun', a children's playground, an 'auto-skooter track', speedboats, 'fully-licensed bars', and a restaurant, café and sun lounge. The West Pier Company, in contrast, seemed unsure of the Pier's identity, trying to cling on to the respectable visitors from the past (Harold Clunn was one) while developing a new funfair market. As the 1930s drew to a close, however, what to do with the Pier was taken out of the hands of the Pier Company.

On 2 September 1939, the day before Britain declared war on Germany and Italy, there was no evening performance in the Theatre because of black-

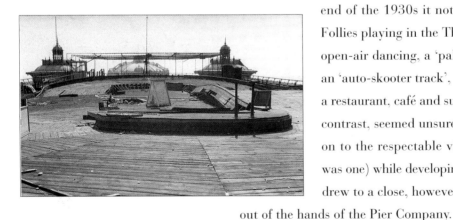

79 ◇ DERELICTION OF WAR: THE ABANDONED MINIATURE RACE TRACK AT THE END OF THE SECOND WORLD WAR

out precautions. This was a temporary upset, and the Pier remained in use during the winter months. In 1939/40 651,000 people visited the Pier. The Theatre was open in March and April 1940 with the Regency Players performing *French Without Tears* and other plays. In late May 'Hitler's Army' had swept through France to the Channel ports and the Pier was taken over by British military authorities on Thursday 23 May. That evening's performance of the appropriately titled *Dangerous Corner*, which had been performed on the Pier in earlier years,

80 ❖ **THE THEATRE AT THE END OF THE WAR**

was cancelled. The scenery and props for the show were rescued two days later by Harold Jack Keates, who was given special permission by the Chief Constable of Brighton Police to visit the Pier 'subject only to any military surveillance that may be considered necessary'. The building never reopened as a theatre.

Although under military control and closed to the public, the Pier management continued its record keeping. An entry in the daily receipt book for August 1940 wistfully (and perhaps in anticipation of government compensation) records: 'Weather generally good in July, rainy spell about 15th for about four or five days, afterwards some cloudy weather, but during the whole of May and June the conditions were perfect for pier business. Hardly any rain fell in August and the conditions again then were ideal. It would have been the best year for bathing in recent times'.

During the summer of 1940 the pier head and landing stages were mined and depth charges laid; the firing point, manned at all times, being in the Concert Hall. It was thought that the Germans lacked shallow draft landing craft and would therefore be forced to use piers and harbours jutting into deeper water to land troops and equipment. In the late summer, with invasion fears mounting, men of the Number 1 Section, 263 Field Company of the Royal Engineers were ordered to cut a 60-foot gap between the pier head and Concert Hall. This work, carried out from mid evening into the early hours of the morning, was achieved by lashing slabs of gun-cotton

81 ❖ **THE WEST PIER COMPANY'S OFFICES STREWN WITH THE CHAOS OF THE SECOND WORLD WAR**

82 ⋄ THE PIER WAS CUT IN TWO
IN 1940 AND THE ISLAND PIER HEAD
BOOBY TRAPPED

83 ⋄ THE MINIATURE MOTOR RACING
TRACK AT THE ENTRANCE OF THE PIER

to each girder in turn, and then retreating to the safety of the Concert Hall to fire the explosives electronically. Numerous journeys were made before a halt was called at 2.30am.

Writing of the events 56 years later, Mr Fred Lynn recalled 'the task was very arduous, because we had to crawl along the centre girder with gun-cotton slabs, primers and detonators stuffed into our denim uniform, together with one of us having the electrical cable tied to the waist and carrying string to lash the slabs to the girders. Also, although we fired the first charge about 21.00hrs., the light soon failed and we had to operate in total darkness.... The night was mild, but very dark and although we could hear the sea gently lapping around the steel piles below us, we could not see the water. Many charges had to be laid because of the depth of the composite girders...each charge meant that we had to make a return journey across the centre girder and then retire to our chosen firing position at the rear of the Concert Hall'. The final central girder was cut later the same morning and the pier head became an island. Within the next few days the original explosives on the pier head were removed and booby traps laid instead.

Three years later, in the autumn of 1943, as the invasion threat eased and the allied forces turned their attention to returning to mainland Europe, the booby traps were removed. Mr Ken Revis, a bomb disposal officer in charge of this work on both Brighton piers, was seriously wounded and blinded as he attempted to remove one of the West Pier mines. After spending a week on his own clearing the Palace Pier of mines under the decking and clusters of gun-cotton in wooden boxes lashed around the legs of the pier, he turned his attention to the West Pier. To get across the gap south of the Concert Hall two pylons of tubular scaffolding were built, one on either side of the gap, which were linked together by a length of rope, a pulley and a sort of bosun's chair. Two teams of two people set about clearing the West Pier, Ken Revis and Corporal Marlowe working on the west side of the Pier.

Speaking more than fifty years later, Ken Revis recalled: 'I had some idea where the mines were. I had a bit of a plan with little blue spots marked on it and also on the deck of the Pier where whoever had laid those mines had put a tiny blue spot which was a bit faded by then. I suppose I had done possibly eight or ten mines which were just under the decking. I used a padsaw to make a slot between the boards of the deck-ing. I took a Corporal with me who at the time of the accident was kneeling behind me. I was in fact kneeling and I was attempting to reach the next mine under where I was. I had just said "Corporal, this is money for old rope", I sort of stretched my back and at that moment up she went. To me it really felt like a boxer being cuffed on both ears at the same time. I can't say it seemed like an explosion because

after all at 8,000 metres per second you haven't much time to know what the hell has happened'. After being taken back across the gap and placed on a stretcher, he was carried to the entrance of the Pier. There 'a girl's voice said "cover his face up" and I remember very clearly shouting out "take the bloody thing off, I'm not dead yet" because I did not want my face covered up when I was on a stretcher'.

In July 1945, shortly after the end of the war in Europe, the national pressure for public control and ownership of the private sector was reflected in the proposal, from some members of Brighton Council, that the Corporation should purchase the West Pier. The chairman of the Entertainments Committee, Councillor Horton-Stephens, said the object was to secure Council control of that part of the seafront. A leading member of the Council, Lewis Cohen, was in favour of the scheme – which included a plan to erect a 'fine bathing pool' at the southern end of the Pier – arguing that 'if Brighton had done something like that before the war we should not then have been faced with a decreasing population, while Bournemouth's population was increasing'. The Council rejected the proposal by 17 votes to five and the issue of it Council ownership of the Pier receded for another quarter of a century.

84 ❖ **THE FUNFAIR PIER FROM THE AIR**

85 ⬧ 'LUNCH AND TEA OVER THE SEA':
THE OCEAN RESTAURANT IN THE
LATE-1940S

With the end of the war the Pier Company set about repairing the considerable damage and decay of the previous five years. It also completed the reshaping of the Pier into a funfair which it had begun before the war. The Company received substantial war compensation from the Ministry of Works: £31,300 in 1946 and a further £78,900 in 1947. The Pier from the root end to the Concert Hall was re-opened to the public on Thursday 18 April 1946, with an opening ceremony taking place the following day, Easter Good Friday. By the beginning of 1948 the whole Pier was open. Although it looked much the same on the outside, inside a rather different pier was to be found.

The greatest change was in the building that had held the Theatre. The removal of the theatre seats and tabs (they were not sold until 1949, the tabs for £160, the seats for £4,900) was confirmation that the Pier's theatrical performances were at an end. Once the theatre furnishings had been taken away a new floor was inserted, dividing the auditorium space. The ground floor became the Games Pavilion housing an indoor funfair with many new attractions including 'Skill Ball', 'Kentucky Derby', children's rides, 'Climbing Monkeys', the 'Rollo Game', and a football game. Other funfair attractions on the Pier included racing cars, bumper cars, a ghost train, kiddies' rides and a shape shifting mirror maze.

Upstairs on the first floor, the relics of Victorian and Edwardian decoration were removed or boarded over, and the space given a plain 'Festival of Britain' make-over, with the curved ceiling enlivened by a painted mural. The new room, with magnificent views of sea and coast, became the Ocean Restaurant. With seats for 700 people, it was advertised with the slogan 'lunch and tea over the sea'. The Concert Hall also took on a different role, being converted to a café with musical performances including afternoon tea dances and dancing in the evenings. The development of the Ocean Restaurant and the Concert Hall café in the Pier's two most important buildings was one of the key decisions taken by the Pier Company after the Second World

86 ⬧ THE POST-WAR CONCERT HALL CAFÉ

War. The expanded food and drink business was run directly by the Company rather than leased to other firms as had been the case before the War.

Many of the attractions on the Pier were run as concessions, contracted or rented out, with the Pier Company receiving either a fixed monthly rent or a share of gross receipts. Between 1946 and 1950 the Company leased space for amusement arcades, fancy goods stalls, shooting ranges, sketch portraits, jockey scales, a shellfish bar, a fruitier and florist, a chemist, and an antiques, curios and bric-a-brac shop. The Pier also hosted 'Recordit Vocal Reproduction', allowing visitors to cut their own records, in much the same way as the one featured in the film *Brighton Rock*, made in the town in 1947. Other businesses used the Pier to sell fishing tackle and bait; for a 'high class jewellers', with articles for sale at a minimum price of £5, 'with the exception of price controlled watches'; and for demonstrations of embroidery and novelties such as gyroscope tops. There were exhibitions, including one of replica Crown Jewels and another, the Richold Collection, of matchstick models of famous buildings.

Some of the traditional pier activities were revived after the War. In 1947 P & A Campbell, the pleasure steamer company, paid £300 for the use of the landing stages by one ship, alternately the *Glen Gower* and the *Empress Queen*. The *Glen Gower* was the last ship operating a regular service from the West Pier along the coast and to France, in 1956. The landing stages were also used for speedboat trips. The bathing station at the pier head was restored, the Pier Company proclaiming the joys of deep water swimming. Professional divers returned to work on the Pier. In the mid-1950s visitors could

88 ❖ PADDLE STEAMER, PROMENADERS AND FISHERMEN USING THE LANDING STAGE

89 ✧ **THE NEW GAMES PAVILION ON THE GROUND FLOOR OF THE CONVERTED THEATRE. THE CEILING SHOWS THE ANGLE OF THE RAKED BALCONY**

watch 'the antics of Professor Javlin, a trick diver at the end of the pier'.

The changes in the Pier after the war were reflected in the Company's major sources of income. For August 1950, tolls and tickets accounted for less than 18 per cent of receipts (it had been over 80 per cent in August 1893 in the last days of the old promenade pier and 34 per cent in August 1920 at the height of the pleasure pier success), the sea-based activities around the pier head (bathing, aquatic entertainments, steamers and speedboats and fishing) just over 12 per cent, the Games Pavilion and other arcades and amusements 35 per cent, and food and drink 31 per cent.

The development of the Pier into an offshore funfair was partially successful in the early post-war years. As with the end of the First World War, peace released the pent-up demand for the pleasures of the English seaside. Speaking in 1997, Peter Marsh, who worked on the Pier from 1947 to 1960, remembered: 'It was busy. People had their money from the army, and for the first five years, this is where people came on holiday. The West Pier was used by people who came on holiday, not for day trippers'. In October 1946 *The Times* reported that 1,250,000 people had visited the West Pier from April to September. But the Palace Pier was massively more successful, 2,144,000 visitors going through the turnstiles from 1 June to 11 October. In 1949/50 1,157,000 people visited the West Pier, although its status as the poor relation to the rival Palace Pier was confirmed, which at about the same time was claiming two and a half million visitors and declaring itself as 'the brightest jewel in Brighton's crown' and, as before the war, 'the finest pier in the world'. By 1952/53, the last year for which records were kept, West Pier admission numbers had fallen to an estimated 900,000 people.

By 1956, and drawing on the success of holiday camps, the Pier was presented as 'a completely self-contained holiday unit on which the visitor to Brighton can spend a first-class holiday without stepping ashore...except to

90 ✧ **ENJOYING THE PIER IN THE EARLY POST-WAR PERIOD**

sleep'. The vestiges of music-making continued in the Concert Hall café with twice daily performances by Harry Groombridge and his orchestra, broadcast over the Pier's loudspeaker system. Harold Clunn's toy cars track was still working inside the Pier entrance 'round which 'youngsters' could 'whirl in brightly-coloured, little petrol-driven cars'. Other 'all the fun of the fair' attractions in 1956 included dodgem cars, a rifle range, a kiddies' roundabout, a ghost train and a crazy maze. The amusement arcades were 'full of the latest automatic machines' – 'all sorts of pin-tables, a group of "What-the-butler-saw" type of peep-shows, punch-ball machines and automatic fortune-tellers'. In the Games' Pavilion side-shows including speedway racing, fishing for toy ducks, and a juke-box – 'the favourite of all teenagers'. The Pier continued to proclaim the attractions of the 'famous Richold Exhibition of architectural and artistic models all carved out of wood' and the Ocean Restaurant remained 'a very popular rendezvous for parties and outings'.

Despite the up-beat presentation of the Pier's attractions in 1956, not much had changed over the ten years since the Pier had re-opened after the War. The Pier Company seemed content to rest on the laurels of post-war transformation rather than respond to the rising living standards and increasing affluence that was to mark the late 1950s and 1960s. The West Pier became ever less successful as a speculative venture. A spiral of decline set in of failing attractions, falling visitor numbers, diminishing income and under-investment. Poor judgements were made about how to meet the challenge of changing holiday demands and the Pier faced intense competition from more successful attractions elsewhere in Brighton, including the Palace Pier. Brighton itself was less successful as a seaside holiday town, at first losing out to holiday areas elsewhere in England and later to the new, accessible and modern Mediterranean resorts. A similar story of post-war difficulties could be told for other English piers. In many resorts, however, piers were demolished or radically altered as owners responded to changing times at the seaside. For the West Pier the relatively gentle decline in the fortunes of the Company (it continued to make a profit in the early 1960s) and a lack of ambition and vision about the

91 ◈

92 ◈

93 ◇ THE BAR OF THE CONCERT HALL CAFÉ, 1960S

94 ◇ STARS OF THE OLDE TYME MUSIC HALL

business meant that the Pier itself survived reasonably well and fundamentally unchanged.

There were, however, some innovations on the Pier during the 1960s. The most successful and well remembered were the summer seasons of *Olde Tyme Music Hall*, produced by Alan Gale, which cast a nostalgic glance backwards. The first show in the Concert Hall opened on 25 June 1964. Each season ran from the end of May or June to October. Bill Pertwee received top billing as 'Your Worthy Chairman' for the 1966 season. The following year Fred Stone took over as chairman, the musical directors were Ken Lyon and Frank Harlow, and the programme featured Gary Webb 'Light Comedian', Patricia Kay 'Soprano', Ricky Lester, Angela Barclay, Sandra McCormick and John Douglass.

Patricia Kay, one of the regular performers and the wife of Alan Gale, recalls how 'we decided to do three different programmes so people staying for a fortnight's holiday could see all three shows, they loved the show and sang along with all the artistes. The Pier was always packed in the sixties, we had people queuing every night almost as far as the Palace Pier. We had numerous celebrities coming each year. Lawrence Olivier, who of course lived in Brighton used to come and sit in the back in disguise. We employed Fred Stone as Chairman, a very well known artiste from the Players Theatre in Villiers Street who of course brought many celebrities into the theatre. Other notable chairmen were Tommy Fields, brother of Gracie Fields, Billy Milton a hugely popular man, Bill Pertwee and Len Howe, comedian'.

Talking over 30 years after the first season, Gary Webb described how *Olde Tyme Music Hall* had started: 'Alan Gale asked me to join him. He said we are going down to do a summer show at Brighton. Alan was good at finding places that had never had a show around the country. He didn't bother with theatres, he wanted places with possibilities, where people could drink, and to sit right the way through and be able to order your pint.

He saw the Concert Hall and thought Oh yes, possibilities. But we had no facilities; from behind where we had the stage, was like the kitchens, but nothing else. So we basically had to build behind there, dressing rooms, and we just partitioned the girls from the boys. We had to build the stage. Alan brought his own tabs down, everyone mucked in. We were an absolute fantastic success, you could not get the people in, so we ran it the next year and ran it through seven years, right till the end, and they were going to close the pier in any case'.

'At the end of the show we would all stand on the stage and it would take three quarters of an hour to say goodnight to everybody, but everybody wanted to say goodnight to you. And it wasn't easy for me, I was in full drag at the end of the show, feathers and everything, trying to bend down to these people. In the summer it was so hot, all glass, you couldn't have the windows open, people outside would have been attracted, and all hell could have broken loose. Of course, seven nights a week, never had a day off, you used to be in there rehearsing, you had to brush up from one programme to another. Very, very hard graft, but very rewarding from our point of view; the audiences were fantastic, you couldn't have paid them to come in and be like that'.

Towards the end of the 1960s, the Pier had another symbolic link with the past and its First World War heyday. It was principal location for the 1969 film *Oh! What a Lovely War*, directed by Richard Attenborough. As if to prove that the Pier Company did not know whether to look to the past or the present, the Pier also featured in the closing beauty contest scenes of *Carry on Girls*.

The last famous West Pier aquatic entertainer, the Great Omani (Mr Ron Cunningham) also enlivened the Pier with many spectacular underwater escapology performances during the 1960s. These included the 'death dive', based on an original Houdini act, and involving jumping into the sea from the pier head hooded, bound and padlocked, and the 'fire dive'. Talking in 1997 the Great

95 ❖ THE PIER IN 1967 DURING THE FILMING OF 'OH! WHAT A LOVELY WAR'. THE SCENE IS SET IN AUGUST 1914

96 ❖ RICHARD ATTENBOROUGH AND JOHN MILLS ON THE SET OF 'OH! WHAT A LOVELY WAR'

Omani said 'it was very simple really, the fire dive. I didn't actually dive, I used to do it as an escapology stunt. I was chained up and I used to jump into the flames. My assistant would throw a half bucket of petrol on to the sea. As it hit the sea it would spread like a fan, and then it would be ignited and it was a very sensational picture because it all went up in a big flame. Of course water magnifies, especially if it is reasonably dusk. At night you get a really big blaze and it looks very spectacular. All I do then is to jump forward right into the centre of the flame. The speed that you are travelling at carries you right through, then you are underwater so you don't really feel the burn but it looks very good. I used to come up again in the middle of it because as you come up the water pushed the fire away'.

'You had to have a very quiet day for it because the wind could sweep the petrol on fire. On one occasion it swept it right under the Pier. The people were standing there and there were shrieks and yells and sparks and smoke were coming up. There was no danger, but that quickly got rid of that audience. One evening I was performing the dive on the West Pier. It was a perfect evening, we had quite a big crowd, it was getting slightly dusk, ideal conditions. The petrol was thrown, my assistant threw the lighted touch onto it and up it blazed. It was a beautiful blaze. Suddenly there was a frantic telephone call through to Daignton, the Pier Manager, from the Manager of the Worthing Pier: "do you know your pier is on fire?", which greatly pleased me because it wasn't on fire but it showed that I had a very large audience'.

Perhaps surprisingly, given the closure of the Theatre, for the first two decades of the post-war period the West Pier Company was controlled by two London impresarios, Tom Arnold and Prince Littler. By the mid-1960s Arnold owned over 16,200 shares and Littler controlled at least 10,500. As 70 years before, the majority of shareholders were local people, although most held no more than one or two hundred shares. But control of the Pier changed suddenly in June 1965. AVP Industries Limited offered 22 shillings for each £1 ordinary share and by June had bought 97 per cent of the shares in the West Pier Company. AVP was a holding company with many other interests including furniture factories, refrigeration and air conditioning, spare parts for watches, and the Metropole and Bedford hotels in Brighton.

Harold Poster, Chairman of AVP and in effective control of the West

Pier Company, announced plans to turn the Pier into a high quality all-year-round holiday and conference attraction, 'giving all the enjoyment of a luxury cruise without any of the discomforts'. While the Victorian features of the structure were to be retained, proposed major redevelopment included a covered and heated central walkway the length of the Pier, a swimming pool and sheltered sunbathing at the pier head, excellent catering and a Palm Court Orchestra. The change in ownership seemed to herald a bright new future for the Pier.

Nothing came of Harold Poster's grand plans. Instead, a complicated sequence of steps over the next decade led not to the revival of the Pier but to its closure.

Rather than radically redevelop the Pier, in the next few years the Company up-graded the funfair. There were new, modern amusements especially at the shore end of the Pier. Tim Gallagher worked on one, the Moonwalker, in 1969. Talking in 1997 he remembers: 'It was quite a revolutionary thing, like a bouncy castle base, top was covered. I think it was in the *Argus*, because it was a new attraction. All inflated by electric motor, it had plastic windows. The problem they had, the seam used to come undone and split, so basically people could fall out. It didn't last very long, not even a season. It ended up with high court writ being served on it because they lost so much money on it. I was eventually subpoenaed to the high court in London, and had to appear in court twice. The bottom line was that the boss I worked for settled out of court, and the company that did the welding was Pacamac, and that year people were buying Pacamacs and they were falling apart'.

Mr Gallagher also worked on the rifle range, owned by a friend's father, 'which was quite fun, had to wear cotton wool in your ears, live ammunition you used – automatic weapons, you gave the punter a clip. There was no restriction on the rifle...You would get a couple of people shooting off, and you had to stand with your back against the counter, facing the customer, and what used to happen people would fire and say this is good, and swing the gun around, and you used to have to knock it out of their hands. 1969 was a particularly bad season, lot of rain. I had a good time, lot of laughs'.

By the late 1960s, Poster and AVP complained about the high cost of maintenance and the damage inflicted by taxes on the Pier activities. In

97 ✧

Above and page 74

98 ✧ **THE PIER IN THE SUMMER OF 1970, WEEKS BEFORE THE PIER HEAD WAS SEALED OFF TO THE PUBLIC**

99 ❖

100 ❖

101 ❖

102 ❖

103 ❖

104 ❖

September 1969 AVP proposed demolishing the landing stage and pier head, promising to spend money redeveloping the Concert Hall and root end of the Pier. In October the Government responded by listing the Pier as a Grade Two building of historic and architectural interest. A year later the pier head was sealed off to the public as unsafe, some of the amusement machines and children's rides being moved to the Concert Hall. In July 1971 the Department of the Environment gave listed building consent for the southern end of the Pier to be demolished, subject to Brighton Council approval and the buildings on the rest of the Pier remaining intact. Amid increasingly vocal campaigns expressing concern for the future of the Pier, in August 1971 AVP offered the Pier to any society that could raise the money to preserve it. None came forward. In the following month Harold Poster proposed that a charitable trust, combining Brighton Council, the Government and AVP, should take over the Pier.

The question of what to do with the Pier went backwards and forwards between the Council and AVP. A survey in January 1974 concluded that at least £1 million was needed to restore the structure, a sum Mr Poster thought it would be commercially unsound for the Company to spend but which was disputed by Pier campaigners. In the succeeding 12 months Brighton Council argued about what to do. During the spring the Planning Committee said the end of the Pier should not be demolished; the Finance Committee recommended saving it; and a chief officer's report emphasised 'its immeasurable architectural and historical importance', also arguing it was second only to the Royal Pavilion among internationally famous buildings in Brighton and Sussex.

In the summer of 1974 there was a debate about whether the Pier should be taken into Council ownership. In December the Policy and Resources Committee recommended the Council should no longer oppose demolition of the seaward end. This decision appeared to be the death knell for the Pier. But it also caused much local and national media interest and a vigorous 'We Want the West Pier' campaign led by people such as John Lloyd (the key person in early years of the West Pier Trust), the actress Judy Cornwell and Councillors Peter Best and John Smith. Although lacking financial resources and formal political power, the campaigners mounted a formidable crusade, which received

105 ✳ WITH THE CLOSURE OF THE PIER HEAD GAMES PAVILION MANY OF THE AMUSEMENTS WERE MOVED TO THE CONCERT HALL

106 ✦ THE FUNFAIR AT THE ENTRANCE OF THE PIER, 1972

107 ✦ A SLEEPY PIER, 1972

great media attention, demanding the retention of the Pier. On 2 January 1975, the Policy and Resources Committee's recommendation was rejected by a full meeting of the Council. Demolition of the West Pier was blocked.

In early July 1975 the West Pier Company declared the whole structure was becoming increasingly unsafe and that the Pier would be closed at the end of the summer season. The author of the *Evening Argus* 'opinion' column on 15 September was in no doubt that 'the conservationists and the council between them must share the blame for turning one of Brighton's major attractions into a derelict site'. For the *Argus* writer the Pier was doomed: 'This is a brutal fact which must be faced. There is no room now for sentiment or airy-fairy plans to raise hundreds of thousands of pounds by public subscription to put this rusting Victorian relic back on its feet'. Within the week, however, the *Argus* reported the results of a study by the 'We Want the West Pier Campaign' that the Pier 'could be restored without a penny from the rates and be turned into a moneyspinner for the council'.

There was stalemate over the future of the Pier. The owners refused to invest in the structure or keep the Pier open; the Council refused to allow demolition but was unwilling to spend public money on it or assume control; the campaigners refused to move from the position that the Pier should be retained and restored in its entirety.

On 30 September 1975 the final visitors paid the eightpence toll to walk on the Pier. Almost exactly 109 years after the grand opening ceremony, the Pier was closed to the public. The equipment that went to make the funfair pier was dismantled and sold. In early December the stock of amusement and gaming machines was bought by a family-owned Folkestone entertainments firm, loaded into lorries and taken to the Rotunda on Folkestone's seafront. All that remained inside the Pier were fragments of the past – books of unsold tickets from the *Olde Tyme Music Hall*, a well-thumbed collection of sheet music used by the members of West Pier Orchestra in the 1920s, dozens of canvas chairs from the Concert Hall café, and a few broken slot machines. The abandoned Pier, forlorn yet defiant and waiting, stood bravely on the water.

108 ✧

EMERGENCY
THEY WANT TO
(on January 2nd, 1975 the full Council will meet and will most probably ratify the decision of the Policy and Resources Committee to—

DESTROY
THE MAIN PART OF THE
WEST PIER
—because, they say, we cannot afford to repair it and put it back into use. **IF YOU DISAGREE** or feel that the people of Brighton should be consulted about such an important issue **SIGN THE**

PETITION
and DEMAND
PUBLIC PARTICIPATION

PETITION FORMS AVAILABLE FROM FORUM GALLERY
16 Market Street, Brighton.   10 a.m. – 5.30 p.m.

109 ✧

041331

Brighton West Pier
CLOSING
SEPTEMBER 30th, 1975

Entire stock of Amusement and Gaming Machines and other equipment to be sold.

Please make application (Principals only) to Anthony G. Webb, Director, Hotel Metropole, Brighton. Tel. Brighton 775432

CHAPTER FIVE

THE CLOSED PIER

Dr Geoff Lockwood, Chief Executive, West Pier Trust

110 ✧ **A VIEW THROUGH THE ROTUNDA AT THE SOUTHERN END OF THE PIER, 1982**

his volume has described the history of the West Pier from its creation to closure to the public in 1975. The history from that closure forms part of the currently incomplete story of the architectural restoration of the Pier and its re-birth as the major social and commercial enterprise it was designed to be.

The Brighton West Pier Trust intends to produce a second volume covering the history since 1975 once the restoration has been completed, but readers of this volume would be dismayed if the story ended in 1975 without indications of what has happened since that time and what the future holds.

111 ◆ THE HOLE LEFT AFTER THE SOUTH-EAST KIOSK PLUNGED INTO THE SEA. FOLLOWING CLOSURE THE SOUTHERN END OF THE PIER WAS MOST AFFECTED BY STORM AND DECAY

The period from 1975 to 1995 falls into three phases. The saving of the Pier from destruction (1975-80), the failing of plans and schemes for its restoration (essentially 1980-89) and the building of a launching pad for the eventual restoration. Each phase is characterised by four features.

The first is the key role of individuals. The fuller history to follow in the second volume will record the very many individuals whose enthusiasm and energy played a part in keeping alive the hope and the potential to restore the West Pier throughout the 20-year long dark age. In this brief contribution, only two of the many can be mentioned, because their roles stand out. If any other name was referred to that would do injustice to dozens of others. John Lloyd takes pride of place as the man whose campaign and subsequent endeavours saved the West Pier from destruction and placed its future in the hands of an independent trust. John is the father of the restored West Pier. Bryan Spielman is to be credited with the commitment and drive which laid the foundations for later. Bryan utilised the partial restoration of the root end of the Pier, stimulated local public confidence in the Trust's ability to restore the Pier and laid the foundations for the bid to the National Lottery. It is gratifying that both men lived long enough to be confident that their Pier would be restored; Bryan died in 1996 and John in 1997. However, it has to be emphasised that theirs was only the major of the very many contributions of individuals in that 20-year period.

Secondly, none of the many initiatives and plans in the period could overcome the basic economic problems of restoring the West Pier. The investment needed to repair the neglected structure was significantly greater than the commercial returns, given the limited deck space of the West Pier (the longer Palace Pier could generate sufficient commercial return for its maintenance). In the economic climate of the 1970s and 1980s there was no national or local public finance available to bridge that gap between the necessary investment and the predictable commercial returns. Throughout that period, the Trust and its supporters were acting on faith against the economic logic.

In the third place, the West Pier suffered from the divisiveness of society and politics in Brighton and Hove into partial and conflicting interest groups. Such divisions were fully reflected within the Trust itself. Brighton and Hove is a cosmopolitan area of major international repute, but in the period under review it was dominated by small town (if not village) politics and cliques. Enthusiasm for the restoration of the West Pier fragmented into very different views about the future nature of the Pier and was faced by outright opposition in other quarters. Such differences resulted in a build-up of cynicism in the town about the ability of any group to achieve the restoration.

Fourthly, there was no one authority, with appropriate professional staff, totally concentrated upon achieving the restoration of the Pier. Various commercial enterprises were involved over that 20-year period, but the West Pier was not central to their interests. The Local Authority had higher priorities than the West Pier. The Trust, with its dedicated amateurs was able to keep alive the hope of restoration, but did not have the unity, resources, standing and professional support necessary to fulfil that hope. Much credit is deserved by English Heritage, without whose steadfast statutory support throughout that period the West Pier might well have not survived. Piers are now recognised as a unique and important part of the British architectural and seaside heritage, but 20-years ago it was far-sighted of English Heritage to award the Grade One listing to the West Pier and to sustain that interest through the failures and despondency that followed.

This summary of the characteristics of the 1975-1995 period inadequately represents the fascinating history, the complicated politics, the economic cycles and conditions, the roles of many authorities and organisations, the persistence of the Trust and the participation of numerous individuals in the West Pier story over those years.

What changed the conditions from 1995? First and foremost, the creation of the National Lottery. As the then Prime Minister, John Major, stated in his 1994 speech to the English Heritage Conference in Brighton, the West Pier was a prime example of the objectives for which the National Lottery had been established. Here, at last, was a source for the funding of the significant gap between the monies needed for the restoration and the level of

112 ◇ THE DESOLATE PIER DURING THE 1980S

113 ✧

114 ✧

115 ✧ DISMANTLING PART OF THE PIER OVER THE BEACH, 1991

investment affordable on a commercial basis. Following discussions with national and local officers, Bryan Spielman selected the path of a submission by the independent Trust to the Heritage Lottery Fund. The bid was for 100 per cent of the costs and it was submitted in June 1995.

At the same time, the British economy was coming out of recession, led by the services sector. Investment in the leisure industry was rising high on the agendas of the major financial houses and companies. Also, by then Brighton Council had begun to cohere around a vision for the regeneration of the town and its economy; returning to the kind of unified and strategic thinking of the Carden era. By 1995, the Council's seafront development initiative was well under way and its geographic line of development was edging towards the West Pier. Both civic vision and the seafront initiative could not ignore the blight of the derelict West Pier. A factor stimulated by the unification of Brighton and Hove Councils in 1997, which placed the West Pier at the central point of the new authority's seafront.

Further, prompted by Bryan Spielman's terminal illness, but springing from the improved climate summarised above, the Trust was strengthened and attracted the professional support needed through a revitalised Board of Trustees, which blended long-serving dedicated members with senior local figures, combining to provide a full range of professional expertise and with major national personalities possessing close interest in the West Pier. Equally important, for the first time in its history, the Trust was able to attract an experienced integrated and professional management team.

If the three phases of the 1975 – 1995 period constitute the main part of the second volume, the story since August 1995 will form at least one fascinating chapter. At the outset the new Chairman (Sir Lindsay Bryson) and I had been led to believe that the Heritage Lottery Fund was poised to provide 100 per cent of the funding for the restoration, and that the lights were set at green in all of the partner and planning authorities for fast track supports and permissions. Suffice it to say that it will have taken nearly three years of unswervingly focused effort, of closely co-ordinated teamwork, of carefully managed public relations and local and national political activity to get all of the lights green at the same time. For too long amber was the favourite colour of the organisations we were dealing with.

The objectives we set in 1995 centred on the faithful restoration of the structure and architecture of the West Pier to its early 1920s appearance (a date chosen partly because the Concert Hall was not completed until 1916 and partly because the Pier was at the height of its popularity at that time). That main objective was surrounded by other key aims.

Firstly, that the Trust itself must have the capacity and strength to fulfil the role of permanent steward of the West Pier. We were not going to hand over the West Pier to a commercial organisation, nor leave it in the control of a small clique. Pursuance of that aim meant that the Trust should remain in direct control of the fundamentals of the Pier. This led to the plan for the Trust to lease the deck of the restored Pier, but to retain responsibility for the sub-structure. It was also argued that the membership of the Trust should be expanded to broaden its roots in the community and amongst the organisations and institutions concerned with the local economy and heritage conservation. In 1995 the membership of the Trust was approximately 250, whereas it passed the 1000 mark by the end of 1997.

116 ☆ INTERIOR OF THE CONCERT HALL, 1996

The second key aim was that the usage and access to the restored West Pier should be true to its tradition. The public should have access to the full length of the Pier so that the historic activities of strolling, fishing, etc, would be maintained. The usage should embrace the artistic, cultural and the educational, rather than just the 'funfair' character of some piers or an 'elite' access to a restored West Pier.

Thirdly, the restored West Pier should blend into, and enhance, the surrounding area as part of the regeneration of the Brighton and Hove seafront. The restoration of the West Pier should have a style or élan which would place the heritage authentically into a twenty-first century society and economy.

Those 1995 objectives remain in place today as the Trust is on the verge of implementing the restoration of the West Pier. To date the progress towards that restoration has been marked most visibly by two physical acts which took

117 ⊹ THE ROOFLESS KIOSK ON THE NORTH-EAST CORNER OF THE PIER HEAD, 1997

118 ⊹ THE EAST SIDE OF THE PAVILION, 1997

place in December 1996. The first was the building of a temporary bridge from the beach to the sea-based sections of the Pier. The stranded Pier was again linked back to land. The storms of 1987 had broken that linkage. The bridge enabled over 2000 people through 1997 to walk on the West Pier to witness its faded glory and to realise its future potential. The second act was the re-illumination of the Pier, aided by Seeboard plc. No event since the 1975 closure had been more symbolic of the determination to restore the Pier. It was a signal, much appreciated by the general public and enthusiasts alike, that the West Pier had returned to life.

The real history of the West Pier since 1975 is the history of the people who have not been able to enjoy its elegance and facilities. All of the local families, tourists, conference delegates and other visitors to Brighton and Hove who have witnessed the derelict state of the Pier and wished that it was whole, alive and accessible. The Trust intends that such despair and disappointment will soon be history.

On the 19th March 1998, the Trustees of the Heritage Lottery Fund agreed, on certain conditions, to accept our application. Thus, on that date the funding for the restoration of the West Pier, public and private, was secured. Now we can get down to the real work. ❧

THE ABANDONED PIER,
ALTHOUGH INCREASINGLY
DECAYED, RETAINED
ITS UNIQUE SPLENDOUR.
PHOTOGRAPHS ON
PAGES 83-85 SHOW
THE PIER IN 1982,
THE REMAINDER IN 1997

119 ☩

120 ✧

122 ✧

123 ❖

124 ❖

125 ❖

126 ❖

127 ❖

128 ❖

129 ❖

130

131

136 ❖

137 ❖

140 ❖

141 ❖

142 ✧

143 ✧

144 ✧

145 ✧

146 ❖

147 ❖